UNLOCKING THE MYSTERIES OF GENESIS

Student Guide

UNLOCKING THE MYSTERIES OF GENESIS

Student Guide

ICR

INSTITUTE FOR CREATION RESEARCH

Dallas, Texas
www.ICR.org

UNLOCKING THE MYSTERIES OF GENESIS

Student Guide

First printing: August 2014

All Scripture quotations are from the New King James Version.

ISBN: 978-1-935587-64-4
Library of Congress: 2014948286

Please visit our website for other books and resources: www.ICR.org

Printed in the United States of America.

Table of Contents

Chaos or Cosmos?

Was the universe designed, or is it a product of random chance?

"The LORD by wisdom founded the earth;
by understanding He established the heavens."
— Proverbs 3:19

What do you see when you look at the world? What do you see in nature? What can you identify in the wings of a butterfly? What do the rising and setting of the sun or the ebb and flow of the tide have in common? To understand how the world came to be—how we came to be—we have to start with the question of design. Design is important. When you consider the world around you—people, atoms, plants, animals, outer space—do you see randomness or design? Did some designer with a purpose and plan execute all that we see and experience? Or was no designer involved and what we see and experience simply happened this way by random processes? It's one or the other. It can't be both.

Brainy Buzzwords

Evidence You Can See

Using the word bank, fill in the blanks. Some words may be used more than once!

adapt	classification	evidence	selections
beautiful	common ancestor	functional	skeletons
bird	complexity	kind	species
Carl Linnaeus	DNA	mimicry	theory of evolution
categories	design	missing	transitional
cats	Designer	natural selection	whale
chameleon	dogs	randomness	

1. When we look at the world around us, do we see _____ or do we see _____?

2. Let's examine a _____'s fin and a _____'s wing. Looking at the _____ of these two, they have a marked similarity. All of Earth's creatures show design that's perfectly suited to where they live.

3. We can group animals, plants, and even minerals into different _____ simply because there are such major similarities. Back in 1735, _____ _____ saved us the trouble of doing it ourselves in his now famous hierarchy of _____.

4. When animals change and adapt to match their surroundings, we call this _____. Like a _____—if he needs to be green, he'll be green. Or brown. Or black. Or whatever he needs.

5. Most scientists see the _____ ___ _____ as the *fact* of evolution. They explain our origins by _____ _____, which says that the animal that is the most fit gets to move up the food chain. And the ones that are the least fit die out.

6. Evolutionists say similarity in Earth's creatures exists because we all came from the same _____ _____ and that through natural selection we adapted features that are similar but unique to our own species.

7. Creation scientists believe that animals and plants must have a _____. There's too much _____ for them to have simply happened randomly.

8. Design is _____, but design is also _____.

9. Creation scientists agree that animals do adapt. But first, they point out that animals _____ only within their own kind—big cats to little _____ and big dogs to little _____. Not from one kind to another _____.

10. Our _____ is the program that runs the machinery of our body.

11. Natural selection is often a misnomer. Nature can't select because the _____ are already designed into each creature's DNA.

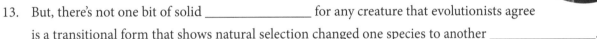

12. In order for naturalistic scientists to get their theory to work, they rely upon one extremely critical bit of evidence—the _____ forms—sometimes called the _____ links.

13. But, there's not one bit of solid _____ for any creature that evolutionists agree is a transitional form that shows natural selection changed one species to another _____.

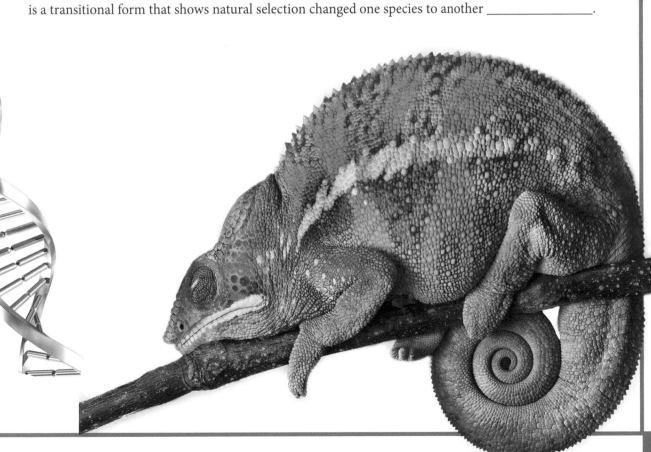

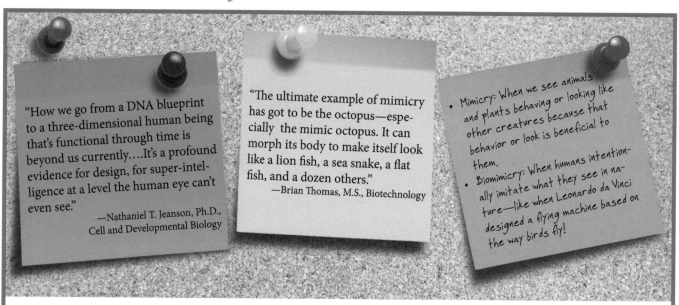

"How we go from a DNA blueprint to a three-dimensional human being that's functional through time is beyond us currently....It's a profound evidence for design, for super-intelligence at a level the human eye can't even see."
—Nathaniel T. Jeanson, Ph.D., Cell and Developmental Biology

"The ultimate example of mimicry has got to be the octopus—especially the mimic octopus. It can morph its body to make itself look like a lion fish, a sea snake, a flat fish, and a dozen others."
—Brian Thomas, M.S., Biotechnology

• Mimicry: When we see animals and plants behaving or looking like other creatures because that behavior or look is beneficial to them.
• Biomimicry: When humans intentionally imitate what they see in nature—like when Leonardo da Vinci designed a flying machine based on the way birds fly!

Think Tank

1. Where do you see design in our world and in your family?

   _____

   _____

2. Why do we see "mimicry" among plants and animals? Give some examples.

   _____

   _____

3. There is a lot of beauty in the world that serves no apparent purpose, but beauty isn't random. So, why do you think it's there?

   _____

   _____

4. What do evolutionists believe about the origin of life?

   _____

   _____

5. Creation scientists agree that animals adapt, but what are two key points on which they disagree with secular scientists?

   _____

   _____

6. Other than experiments, what important evidence do evolutionists need to support their theory about the origin of life, and where is this evidence?

   _____

   _____

7. Can you think of a time when it would have been helpful to explain where life came from? How can you prepare to answer questions about origins in the future?

   _____

   _____

Extraordinary Evidence

Most scientists take evolution as a fact not as a theory. They believe in random forces and natural selection. Check out this scientific evidence that challenges an evolutionary origin and points to God's creation:

Our Atmosphere

Today's atmosphere contains 78 percent nitrogen (N_2), 21 percent molecular oxygen (O_2), and one percent of other gases, like carbon dioxide (CO_2), argon (Ar), and water vapor (H_2O). An atmosphere that had free oxygen (oxygen atoms not bonded to any other atoms) would be fatal to all origin of life schemes—it would oxidize and destroy all organic molecules required for life to start. Even though there is much evidence that the earth has always had a huge amount of free oxygen in the atmosphere, evolutionists keep saying that there was no oxygen in the earth's early atmosphere. But *this would also be fatal to the way evolutionists say life began.*

Without oxygen, there wouldn't be a protective layer of ozone surrounding the earth. The sun's deadly, destructive ultraviolet light would pour down on the surface of the earth with nothing stopping it, destroying the organic molecules required for life.

Evolutionists face a problem they can't solve: In the presence of oxygen, life could not evolve; but without oxygen (which means no ozone), life could not evolve…or exist.

Fun Fact: Did you know there are over a million species of living things? And others still undiscovered!

Raw Energy Is Destructive!

The energy available on a hypothetical primitive earth would include mostly radiation from the sun, with some energy from electrical discharges (lightning) and minor sources of energy from radioactive decay and heat. Evolution's problem is that sources of raw energy destroy biological molecules faster than sources of raw energy form them. The fast breakdown of those supposed "building blocks" of life would remove any possibility of them accumulating enough organic compounds to make life—no matter how much time might be available.

Micromolecules Don't Randomly Make Macromolecules

Evolutionists keep claiming that the first stage in the origin of life was the origin of a self-replicating DNA or RNA molecule. There is no such thing as a self-replicating molecule.

The formation of a molecule requires the input of a precisely selected type of energy and the steady input of the building blocks required to form it. For example, to produce a protein, the building blocks are amino acids. Nucleotides are the building blocks of DNA and RNA.

But if amino acids are dissolved in water they don't spontaneously join together to make a protein. That would require adding energy. If proteins are dissolved in water, the chemical bonds between the amino acids slowly break apart, releasing energy.

To form a protein in a laboratory, chemists must dissolve the required amino acids in some solvent other than water and then add a chemical that contains high-energy bonds. This provides the necessary energy to form the chemical bonds between the amino acids and releases hydrogen and hydroxide to form water. This only happens in a chemistry lab or in the cells of living organisms. It could never have taken place in a primitive ocean or anywhere on a primitive earth.

Adapted from Morris III, H. M. 2009. *Exploring the Evidence for Creation.* Dallas, TX: Institute for Creation Research.

For more extraordinary evidence, check out Guide to Creation Basics *at the ICR.org store!*

Back to the Bible

"O LORD, how manifold are Your works!
In wisdom You have made them all.
The earth is full of Your possessions."
— Psalm 104:24

Read

Genesis 1:1-28 • Psalm 104:24 • Proverbs 3:19 • Isaiah 14:24 • Romans 1:20 • Ephesians 2:10

Respond

1. According to the Bible, how long did God take to create everything?_____

2. What happened on each day? _____
   _____
   _____

3. What did God think about His creation? _____

4. What commands did God give to His creation and also specifically to man?_____
   _____
   _____

5. When God created man, what did He do differently than He did with His other creations? _____
   _____
   _____

6. What do these verses tell us about who God is? _____
   _____
   _____

7. How can you recognize the Designer who made you? How can you walk in the works that He has purposed for you? _____
   _____
   _____

Takeaways

The Bible describes our complex world with a simple explanation that accounts for everything: Our world was made by a Designer. In the first chapter of Genesis, God laid out for us the steps He wisely took when He created the world. He planned and purposed our world—and YOU!

Awesome Activities for All Ages

1. Family art project

   As a family: Head outdoors—either to your own front yard or to a local park or arboretum. Have students spread out and create chalk or sketchbook drawings of things they can see in nature that show design. Give everyone a chance to share their final masterpiece and talk through the design elements they found in nature!

2. Creation chart

   As a family: Work together to make a creation chart mapping out the days of the creation week.

   Younger students: Use art supplies for the chart that are age appropriate—finger paint, crayons, or markers—or cut and paste pictures from magazines.

   Older students: Draw original illustrations for the chart, and write detailed descriptions of what happened on each creation day.

3. The atmosphere

   As a family: Talk about the atmosphere that is required for life and how this affects the evolutionary theory.

   Younger students: Learn about oxygen and the right amount and intensity of sunlight and how they are important for life. Plant a seed in a small window pot; care for and observe the growth process that requires water, oxygen, and sunlight.

   Older students: Write a one-page persuasive paper using outside research resources to explain how oxygen presents an unsolvable problem for evolutionary origins. Present your findings to the group.

4. Field trip

   As a family: Schedule a field trip to a fire station or auto mechanic's shop and ask an expert to talk about how different equipment parts work together because of design not random chance.

5. Driving tour

   As a family: Drive through your city and identify creative architecture. Talk through everything that went into designing these buildings and why they could not just happen to form.

6. Origami animals

   As a family: Consider the mimic octopus described in Episode One. What does it take to mimic another creature? Find out for yourself by making an origami animal of your choice. Purchase an origami kit online or from a local art or bookstore. Follow the kit instructions to create an origami animal, and then compare your paper creation to a picture of the real animal you chose to "mimic." Discuss your answers to these questions:

   a. In what ways do the origami animals differ from the real animals? How are they similar?

   b. What human characteristics or abilities did making paper imitations require (ex: intelligence, perseverance, ability to read instructions, logic, intent, etc.)?

   c. How does your ability to copy real creatures with paper compare to what the mimic octopus does when it copies creatures in real life—who is a better "mimic"? Describe the abilities required to create a real animal like the mimic octopus that can copy other animals so well.

2

Episode

What Is Life?

One of the biggest questions we face is "What is life?"—what we believe about this matters.

"And God made the beast of the earth...and everything that creeps on the earth according to its kind. And God saw that it was good."
— Genesis 1:25

Whether you assume that life is the product of chance and time or that God created life in its current form—or you believe a little bit of each—the question remains: What is life? You can take a clinical approach and describe life by the biological functions and processes that take place, or you can describe the basic chemical elements that distinguish plants and animals from inorganic matter like rocks. But this still doesn't get at the big question. What is that breath of God or spark of energy or whatever you want to call it—that thing that starts life and ends at death?

Brainy Buzzwords

Alive or Not?

Circle each item on this list that scientists would classify as being biologically and biblically alive.

horse

algae

roly poly

tree

mushroom

telephone pole

rabbit

cow

mountain

girl

tomato

butterfly

rock
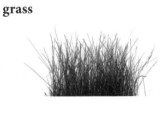

squash

cave

grass

lion

ocean

bumble bee
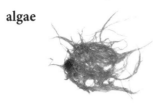

shark
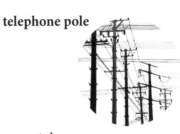

rose

Brainy Buzzwords

Know Your Terms!

Match each term to its definition.

1. _____ Life

2. _____ Primordial soup model

3. _____ Vertical evolution

4. _____ Second Law of Thermodynamics

5. _____ First commandment to humans

6. _____ First Cause

a. Over time, creatures move upward from the simplest creature to the most complex.

b. That which came before the universe and created the universe

c. "Be fruitful and multiply; fill the earth and subdue it; have dominion."

d. The ability to grow, reproduce, move independently, and metabolize

e. Random chemicals came together and formed the first self-replicating molecule.

f. Everything tends to go from order to disorder.

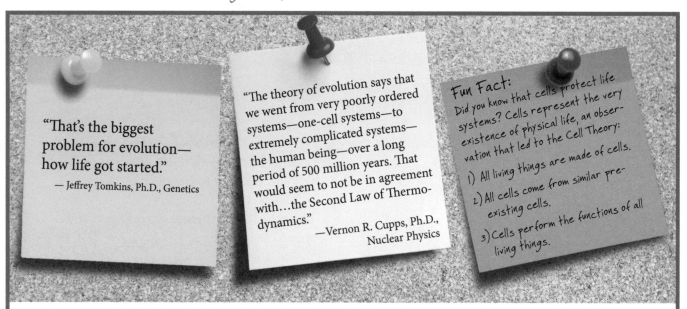

"That's the biggest problem for evolution—how life got started."
— Jeffrey Tomkins, Ph.D., Genetics

"The theory of evolution says that we went from very poorly ordered systems—one-cell systems—to extremely complicated systems—the human being—over a long period of 500 million years. That would seem to not be in agreement with…the Second Law of Thermodynamics."
—Vernon R. Cupps, Ph.D., Nuclear Physics

Fun Fact:
Did you know that cells protect life systems? Cells represent the very existence of physical life, an observation that led to the Cell Theory:
1) All living things are made of cells.
2) All cells come from similar pre-existing cells.
3) Cells perform the functions of all living things.

Think Tank

1. What are some characteristics scientists look for to decide if something is alive?

   _____

   _____

2. What does the Bible say about the origin of life and man's responsibility in the world?

   _____

   _____

3. What are three "mechanisms" that evolutionists think took creatures from being simple to being complex? _____

   _____

4. What are some problems with the theory of evolution? _____

   _____

   _____

5. What was the significance of Louis Pasteur's origin of life experiments? _____

   _____

6. What clue does Genesis 1:11-12 give about how organisms reproduce? And what does it suggest about DNA?

   _____

   _____

7. If someone believes life started just with chemicals randomly fitting together, how does that affect their worldview?

   _____

   _____

8. Think of someone you know who might have a view on origins that is not based on the Bible. How would you support the fact that life only comes from life?

   _____

   _____

Extraordinary Evidence

Life Was Created Fully Functional

Many impossible things would have to happen for evolution to explain where life came from. The most logical explanation is that a First Cause—something all-powerful (omnipotent) and all-knowing (omniscient) beyond our universe—created life.

DNA Points to a Creator

DNA, Deoxyribonucleic acid, is the information system for life. This complex language system stores life's blueprints and demands an author. Information is a product of intelligence, which indicates that DNA came from an intelligent source, the Creator.

> **Fun Fact:**
> Biogenesis: The theory that life only comes from similar pre-existing life and not from nonliving material or unrelated life forms. The Bible tells us that ultimately all life came from Christ (John 1).

Cells Protect Life Systems

All living things are made of cells. For DNA and proteins to work correctly, the cell membrane must protect them from unwanted reactions with chemicals in the environment. Proteins provide the catalyst for building and maintaining this wall-like barrier, and DNA's information specifies the construction of those proteins. In the end, the cell membrane selects materials helpful to the cell and protects it against harmful ones. These three factors—DNA information, protein catalysts (enzymes), and a protective environment—have to be present at the same time for life to exist as cells.

Natural Selection and Adaptation Don't Create Life

Changes in basic kinds of organisms are limited to variations within the kinds. Harmful mutations lead to extinction not to new complex systems. Mutations cannot *create* a single gene. Plants and animals were originally created with large gene pools within their created kinds. A large gene pool gives a created kind the genetic potential (the potential to produce a variety of types within a kind) to adapt to different ecosystems and ensure the survival of that kind of organism. For example, there are many shapes, sizes, and colors of dogs, illustrating the tremendous genetic potential in this kind of animal. Natural selection can only operate on the genetic material already present in a population of organisms of the same kind. It can't *create* new genetic information and then change one kind of organism into another—it can't change a dog into a cat.

Life's Natural Direction Is Not Evolution

Copying errors in DNA's information are called mutations, which adversely affect the cell and organism. Damage to the genome shortens the lifespan of individuals and entire populations. As time passes, genetic information erodes. Mutations in the genomes of organisms are usually nearly neutral, with little effect on the organism's fitness—its ability to survive. But the buildup of harmful mutations does occur, and this causes genetic degeneration. Mutations lead to the loss of genetic information and, consequently, the loss of genetic potential. This results in what is termed genetic load for a population of organisms. Genetic load is the amount of mutation in a kind of organism that affects its fitness in a particular environment. We haven't seen mutations increase genetic potential, but they do increase genetic load and make survival harder—especially in man. So life naturally heads toward harmful changes, not the helpful ones that evolution claims.

Adapted from Morris III, H. M. 2009. *Exploring the Evidence for Creation*. Dallas, TX: Institute for Creation Research.

For more extraordinary evidence, check out Guide to Creation Basics *at the ICR.org store!*

Back to the Bible

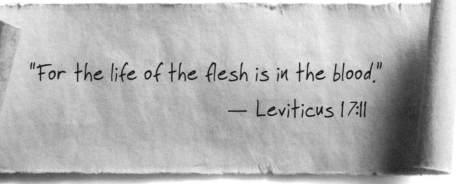

"For the life of the flesh is in the blood."

— Leviticus 17:11

Read

Genesis 1:26, 28-29 • Leviticus 17:11 • 1 Corinthians 15:20-26

Respond

1. What does it mean when the Bible says life is "in the blood"? How does this fit with how scientists would describe something as alive? _____
    _____

2. Where did all of life come from? _____

3. List some things that set humans apart from plants and animals. _____
    _____

4. What important task did God give us in Genesis? _____
    _____

5. If we truly believe that God made us special and set apart, how should that change the way we work, play, live, and interact with others? _____
    _____

6. What hope do Christians have in spite of the fact that life will someday end?
    _____
    _____

Takeaways

-   From God's record in Genesis, we learn exactly how the world was created, where life came from, and the many purposes of His creation.

-   Each animal was made to fill its own niche in the world. All their abilities are encoded into their unique DNA, but only man was created in God's image—with this comes responsibility for the world around us and a special decision for how we will relate to our Creator when it comes to salvation.

-   If life starts with just chemicals randomly aligning, then the end of life is nothing more than another set of chemical reactions changing our bodies back into dust. Our life doesn't really have meaning. But if we believe that God is the source of life and we trust in Jesus as His Son, then we'll have eternal life with God and purpose for every day!

Awesome Activities for All Ages

1. Creation's purpose

   As a family: Read Genesis 1:1-28 out loud. Talk through the different purposes for animals, plants, and humans. On a white board, list out the way everything's unique purpose should affect how we live within our world and treat each other. Decide on a family covenant of some things you can do to better treat each other like people who are created in God's image.

   Younger students: Color and illustrate each part of the "family covenant" in a mini-booklet or on a chart. Reward them with stickers throughout the week each time they show regard for God's creation—for example, picking up trash, saying a kind word, or helping with chores.

   Older students: Using your history curriculum or current fiction or nonfiction reading assignment, select two quotes or a passage showing contrasting ideas about man's role in society. Compare these viewpoints in a one- or two-page essay, using the Bible as a supporting resource.

2. Petting zoo

   As a family: Visit a petting zoo where students have the opportunity to see animals in all life stages.

   a. What physical attributes (structures) do you see?

   b. What is the purpose of each physical feature (function)?

   c. What does the relationship between structure and function tell us about design?

   d. Identify differences between a baby creature's body and an adult's body. How do these illustrate a purpose and plan?

3. Watch it grow

   As a family: Combine one tablespoon of sugar with 1/4 cup of water in a tall glass. Then, add one teaspoon of yeast. Mark the fluid level on the outside of the glass and watch the organisms produce froth as they grow, raising the fluid level. Meanwhile, research basic cell functions. Discuss the precise design requirements of single-cell organisms like yeast that show how they are not "simple." Answer these questions:

   a. What steps does a cell need to take in order to feed on the sugar in solution?

   b. What kind of machinery might the cell use to detect or discern sugar from other chemicals in its environment?

   c. What kind of machinery might the cell use to import the sugar into itself while keeping other chemicals out?

   d. How could you describe the machinery that is able to capture chemical energy from within sugar molecules and transfer that energy into cell growth and reproduction, all at room temperature?

   e. The froth is formed from CO_2 gas, a byproduct of oxidizing sugar. What are the chances that single-cell yeast organized its own internal chemistry labs?

3 Episode

What Is Man?

One of the most controversial questions in all of science centers on where humans came from. Did we evolve from the animal kingdom, or were we uniquely and divinely created to be stewards over the earth?

"Then God said, 'Let Us make man in Our image, according to Our likeness; let them have dominion over the fish of the sea, over the birds of the air, and over the cattle, over all the earth and over every creeping thing that creeps on the earth."

— Genesis 1:26

Have you ever wondered where we came from? Is it true that the earth is billions of years old and that humans have only been around a fraction of the time? Are people just intelligent animals, or are we more special than that? What makes us human, and what is our purpose?

Brainy Buzzwords

What's the Same and What's Different?

Circle the things on the mare and the foal that are the same. Draw a square around the things that are different.

1. What are some physical characteristics you have that are just like your mom and dad?

    _____

    _____

2. What are some physical characteristics that make you different from your mom and dad?

    _____

    _____

Brainy Buzzwords

Cracking the Genetic Code

Using the word bank below, fill in the blanks. Some words may be used more than once!

23	blueprint	gene	macromolecule	paragraphs
A	characteristics	generation	molecule	parent
C	chromosome	genetic	mother	physical
G	DNA	grandparents	nucleus	sentences
T	diseases	hair	one-cell	tall
X	function	human	organism	zebra
Y	gender	ladder	pair	

1. The key to what we are biologically—whether we're a person or an amoeba or a chimpanzee or a gnat—is written in the _____. It's the _____ of our bodies.

2. DNA is a _____ found in the _____ of nearly every cell of every living thing. The DNA tells the cell what _____ to do.

3. The DNA is packed tightly together to make a _____; each chromosome carries information in the form of many _____s.

4. Inside the _____ is the heredity information that is passed from _____ to generation.

5. This information helps determine _____ attributes like your _____ color, how _____ you might grow, your facial _____, and even whether and when you will you lose your _____.

6. And on the most basic level, your DNA carries the information that determines what kind of _____ you are. All organisms get their DNA information from their parent or _____s, whether it's a _____ mold spore, a bear, or a human.

7. In humans, you get _____ chromosomes from your _____ and 23 from your father. The smallest of those pairs of chromosomes—the ____ and ____ chromosomes—determines your _____, among other things. The other 22 pairs of chromosomes carry your other _____ makeup and even your predisposition to certain _____.

8. And, of course, each of your parents received their attributes from their _____s. And your _____ got theirs from your great-grandparents. And they, in turn, got their attributes from their parents, your great-great-_____.

9. A DNA _____ has a double-helix structure that looks like a twisted _____. The ladder's rungs are made from four unique chemicals called nucleotides, known by their initials ____, ____, ____, and ____. They _____ up—A with T and G with C—all along the DNA strand.

10. The DNA strand is made of these four chemical letters. Those letters make _____ words. Those words form genetic _____, and those sentences make _____. In this analogy, genes are the sentences and _____s are the paragraphs.

11. A creature's particular DNA sequence of chemical letters is what determines what the _____ is—whether it's a jellyfish or a _____, a butterfly or a _____!

"We find that the dexterity that people have, compared to chimpanzees, is a lot more detailed, a lot more complex."

— Frank Sherwin, M.A., Zoology

"The differences are too vast for evolution to work...for us to evolve from a chimp-like creature or a primate. It's just not possible—the genomes are that different."

— Jeffrey Tomkins, Ph.D., Genetics

"The difference between human beings and animals does not boil down to biology. We are not just more sophisticated animals.... You have infused in you the image of God."

— Randy Guliuzza, P.E., M.D.

Think Tank

1. Name two influential evolutionists and discuss how they changed the relationship between science and theology and promoted evolutionary theory.

   _____

   _____

2. What are evolution's basic assumptions?

   _____

   _____

3. What are some flaws with the theory that the genomes and anatomy of chimps and humans are similar enough to indicate they shared a common ancestor?

   _____

   _____

4. What are three main problems with the theory of evolution?

   _____

   _____

5. How do "irreducibly complex" systems support creation?

   _____

   _____

6. List at least five aspects that separate humans from animals. What is the biggest characteristic God gave humans that sets us apart from animals, and what does this quality enable us to do?

   _____

   _____

7. Why does our view on human origins matter?

   _____

   _____

8. How would you explain the value of human life to someone who believes we are no more than sophisticated animals?

   _____

   _____

Extraordinary Evidence

Humans had a beginning—when and what was it? What makes us unique and so much more than highly evolved animals at the top of the food chain?

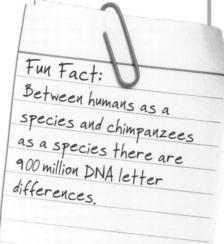

Fun Fact:
Between humans as a species and chimpanzees as a species there are 900 million DNA letter differences.

Created in His Image—Recently and Miraculously

The first human beings didn't evolve from an animal but were specially created in fully human form from the start. Genesis 1 says that God created man in His image, a quality that separates us from the animals created on Day Six. This special creation explains why our behavior is far more complex than any other living thing on the planet. We reveal God's image in many ways—like being able to imagine and make objects never seen before, being able to show compassion for strangers, and being able to ponder our role and fate in creation.

Man also has a different relationship to God from the other creatures. Man was created to serve other men and God, a fact that forms the basis for society. We are God's most treasured creation—so much so that He created us in His image and died to reconcile us to Himself. This value that God places on us truly separates humans from the rest of creation.

Without Repair Mechanisms DNA Could Not Survive

For life to exist, an information system—DNA—is needed to produce and regulate life functions. But DNA can be destroyed by a variety of agents, including ultraviolet (UV) light, reactive oxygen species, alkylating agents, and water. Yes, even water can damage DNA! So, water and many chemical agents dissolved in it, along with UV light, would destroy DNA much faster than any possible natural process could produce it.

Thank goodness for human DNA repair genes! There are over 100 of them, and without them DNA couldn't survive even in a cell's protective environment. DNA is necessary for the survival of DNA! Therefore, it would have been impossible for DNA repair genes to evolve before ordinary DNA evolved, and it would have been impossible for ordinary DNA to evolve before DNA repair genes had evolved. This is another example of irreducible complexity and an impossible problem for evolution to overcome or explain.

Humans Are Stewards with Purpose and Accountability

Societies demonstrate and understand that humans dominate the earth, ruling over animals, plant life, and the physical environment, just like God said it should be in His dominion mandate (Genesis 1:28). Man has dominion over the earth, but that dominion cannot exceed the boundaries of God's laws—we are stewards of God's creation.

Adapted from Morris III, H. M. 2009. *Exploring the Evidence for Creation*. Dallas, TX: Institute for Creation Research.

For more extraordinary evidence, check out Made in His Image *at the ICR.org store!*

Back to the Bible

"So God created man in His own image; in the image of God He created him; male and female He created them."

— Genesis 1:27

Read

Genesis 1:27 • Romans 5:8 • Philippians 2:13

Respond

1. What did God do differently in His creation of humans compared to animals?

   _____

2. How does God show His love for us? _____

   _____

3. How is our relationship with God different from His relationship with animals?

   _____

   _____

4. Describe what it means for God to be working in us. What does that look like in our everyday lives?

   _____

   _____

5. What ultimate thing gives humans meaning and purpose? _____

   _____

6. What happens when people don't understand their humanity as God tells us He created it in the Bible?

   _____

   _____

Takeaways

- Humans are created in God's image with the unique ability to have a spiritual life and genuine, intelligent, compassionate fellowship with God forever.

- God put Adam and Eve on Earth as stewards of His creation.

- Humans have ultimate meaning and purpose because we are created in God's image to have fellowship with Him forever, and that relationship has been redeemed by the death and resurrection of Jesus Christ. That is how important we are to God, and that should give us joy, hope, and purpose every day.

Awesome Activities for All Ages

1. Zoo trip

As a family: Take a family field trip to the zoo! Take sketch pads and crayons and spend some time at the chimpanzee viewing area. Draw or list as many observations as you can about chimpanzees. Discuss similarities and differences between chimps and humans. Does similar design indicate a common ancestor? Why or why not?

Younger students: Using drawings and photos from the field trip, create a scrapbook journal of your day at the zoo.

Older students: Choose a particular species to research. Create a zoo guide, including important facts, pictures, and warnings for guests. Be creative in the formatting—for example, develop a pamphlet or a poster or even a plaque that would hang outside the animal's habitat.

2. Scopes trial

As a family: Read a synopsis of the Scopes trial from ICR.org. What was the significance of the outcome for society's view of origins?

Older students: Research the trial in more detail, reviewing the new evidence we have today. Watch the film *Inherit the Wind*. Based on your research, did Hollywood accurately portray the facts of the trial? Discuss any agendas that may have motivated the production of this film.

3. Created in His likeness

As a family: Discuss what it means to be created in someone's likeness. How is this similar to or different from being created in God's image?

- Sort through photo albums, pick a favorite family picture, and recreate your own version using any medium you would like.

- Date and frame each work of art, hang them for display, and have an art show. Have each artist share why they chose their particular picture and art medium and the similarities and shared traits they included in their portrait.

- End the presentation by talking about how each piece of artwork shows that the artists are unique and how the fact that they can rationally think and create shows they were created in God's image.

4. Morality

As a family: Discuss different scenarios involving moral choices.

- Has a favorite toy or object of yours ever been taken from you? How did it make you feel? Have you seen anyone's things taken from them? How did the owner react?

- Try to steal your dog's, cat's, fish's, iguana's, or any other pet's favorite toy while the animal is not playing with it. Even if you promise to never return it to them, do they react the same way as a person would? Why or why not?

- Examine Job 35:11 in the light of Genesis 1:26. How do these verses help explain why people react differently from animals when wrongs are committed against them or others?

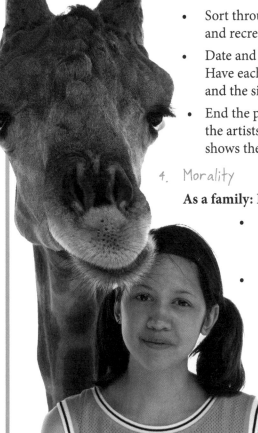

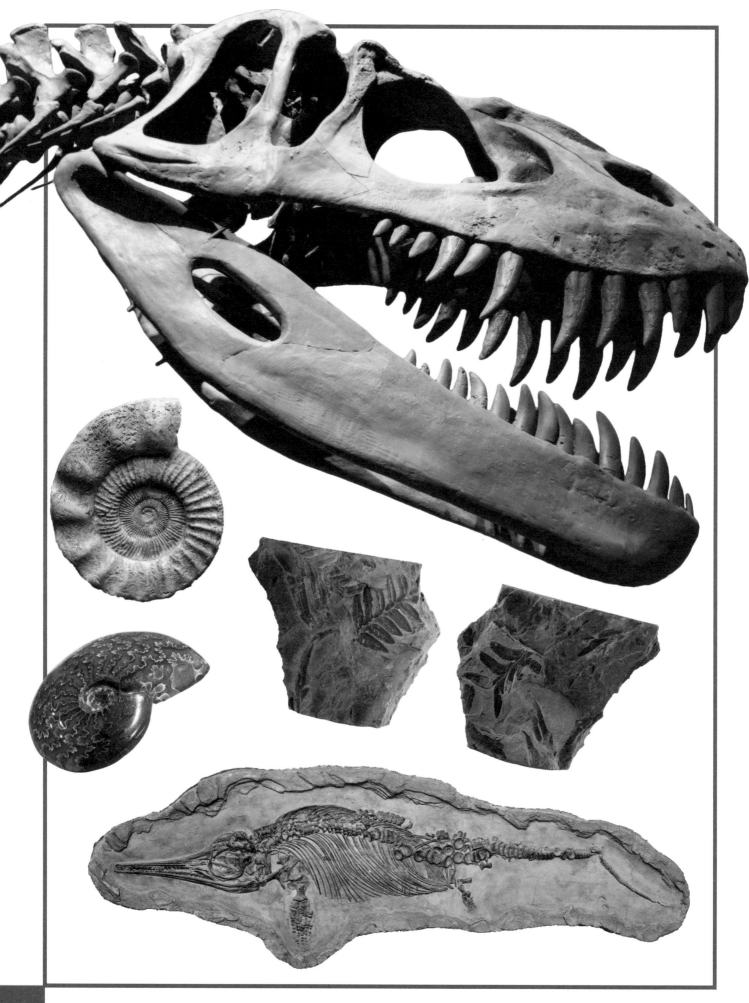

4
Episode

Buried Clues

Fossils are the only hard evidence that can help us understand what life existed in the distant past. What secrets do they reveal, and what can science really tell us?

"And the waters prevailed exceedingly on the earth, and all the high hills under the whole heaven were covered....And all flesh died that moved on the earth: birds and cattle and beasts and every creeping thing that creeps on the earth, and every man."
— Genesis 7:19, 21

Can science, along with the Bible, really provide answers for the deepest questions of life? There is a way of digging up the evidence—and finding the truth. Fossils are like snapshots of the past that give us a glimpse of the abundant life that once populated the earth. But do they explain the origins of that life? What do fossils actually show us?

Brainy Buzzwords

Finding the Missing Links

See how quickly you can find all of these words hidden in the puzzle below! Words may be spelled vertically, horizontally, diagonally, or backward.

ARCHAEOPTERYX
BURIAL
CAMBRIAN
COMPLEX
DARWIN
DINOSAUR
EVIDENCE
EXPLOSION

FOSSILS
GEOLOGY
GRAND CANYON
INVERTEBRATE
LIFE FORM
MISSING LINKS
MUDFLOW
ORGANISM

SIMPLE
SNAPSHOT
SOFT TISSUE
STASIS
STRATA
TRANSITIONAL

```
I G L M E S S E V I D E N C E
O R G A N I S M O D T M E U S
L A N O I T I S N A R T S O T
S N A P S H O T R L N S I E R
W D N V A R S B N A I C B N A
M C E O I S E N C T H A H I T
E A O E I T D O T I O M R B A
L N C R R S M F G E A B U S O
X Y R E T P O E A H C R A M A
A O V A L S O L D S I I S U T
R N S E S L P A P A L A O D R
I I X I O F R R L X R N N F O
S H L G C W M R O F E F I L D
C S Y S I M P L E P O V D O N
D S K N I L G N I S S I M W O
```

Brainy Buzzwords

Buried Evidence

Using the word bank below, fill in the blanks. Some words may be used more than once!

another	decay	fossils	shift
burial	deeper	important	simple
buried	diversity	layers	slow
change	earth	organism	thousands
complex	evidence	rapid	transitional
complexity	evolved	record	upper

1. One of the main tools evolutionary scientists have used to promote evolution has been the fossil record—all the _____ that lie buried in rock formations in Earth's sedimentary _____, or strata. As you go deeper into the _____, the common assumption is that you go _____ in time.

2. When you look at which _____ are buried in which layer, evolutionists say you supposedly get a picture of how life _____ from the simplest organisms _____ in the deepest layers, to more _____ and recent organisms, like dinosaurs, in the _____ layers. Most evolutionists believe that this process of animals developing from _____ to complex was a very _____ and gradual one.

3. If change happened very gradually, there should theoretically be transitional forms in the fossil _____ that show a major body _____ between early versions of an _____ and more complex later versions.

4. But so far no undisputed _____ fossils have been found. So what does the _____ show?

5. Exhibit A: Diversity

   The evidence indicates a tremendous _____ of life, thousands upon _____ of examples of fossils—all preserved with few, if any, signs of decay. How could this happen? Dead animals don't usually turn into _____. So what forces could have created such near-perfect preservation? A very _____ burial of these creatures provides an explanation—a _____ so rapid that they didn't have time to _____ or end up as dinner for scavengers.

6. Exhibit B: Stasis (Stability)

   The fossil record contains fully formed, plentiful life that shows _____ and completeness without major _____—therefore, stability. And, strangely enough, the supposed _____ forms of life are missing. Amid all the diversity and complexity of fossils, there is no undisputed _____ creature that shows one species transitioning into _____.

7. It looks like what the fossil record *doesn't* reveal could be just as _____ as what it does.

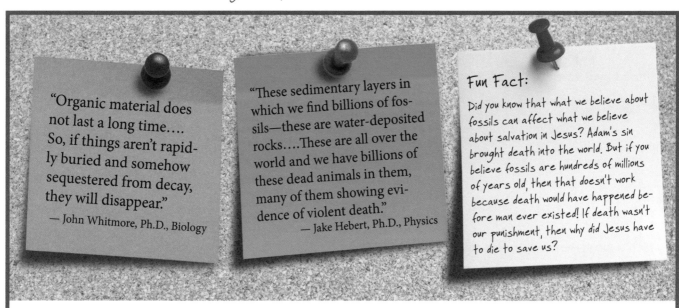

"Organic material does not last a long time.... So, if things aren't rapidly buried and somehow sequestered from decay, they will disappear."
— John Whitmore, Ph.D., Biology

"These sedimentary layers in which we find billions of fossils—these are water-deposited rocks....These are all over the world and we have billions of these dead animals in them, many of them showing evidence of violent death."
— Jake Hebert, Ph.D., Physics

Fun Fact:
Did you know that what we believe about fossils can affect what we believe about salvation in Jesus? Adam's sin brought death into the world. But if you believe fossils are hundreds of millions of years old, then that doesn't work because death would have happened before man ever existed! If death wasn't our punishment, then why did Jesus have to die to save us?

Think Tank

1. Name one of the main tools evolutionists use to promote evolution. How does this method supposedly give a picture of how life evolved?

   _____

2. Why do evolutionists say there should be buried transitional forms?

   _____
   _____

3. Why would some say that evolution is a religion? Do you agree? Why or why not?

   _____
   _____

4. Two characteristics of the fossil record are diversity and stasis. Why are these significant?

   _____
   _____

5. What is the big difference between the rock layers known as Precambrian and Cambrian? How does this connect to how evolutionists explain the gaps or unconformities in the geologic strata—for example, at Grand Canyon?

   _____

6. What organisms make up the majority of fossils? What kinds of organisms are found the least in the fossil record?

   _____

7. What event in Earth's past best explains how fossils were buried and where they are found?

   _____
   _____

8. What do soft tissue fossils indicate?

   _____

9. Name two scientists who were mocked for their ideas but ended up being right. What can you learn from their decisions to stand by their beliefs? Has there been a time when you knew you were right but it cost you something?

   _____
   _____

Extraordinary Evidence

What can we learn about the past from looking at fossils?

Stasis, Not Transitional Forms

The creation model for the fossil record predicts: 1) abrupt appearance, 2) complexity of organisms at all levels of rock layers, and 3) stasis—no change in organisms' defining characteristics. Evolutionary models for the fossil record predict: 1) change of organisms through time, 2) primitive organisms giving rise to complex organisms, and 3) gradual development of new organisms, producing transitional forms. A careful scientist would use these predictions to evaluate the evidence and determine which model is the most correct.

Immediate Appearance of Complex Life

When a fossil appears in the sedimentary rock layers, it appears fully developed, with no evidence for a transitional ancestor at all. For instance, fish have no ancestors or transitional forms that show how invertebrates, with their skeletons on the outside, became vertebrates with internal skeletons. Fossils of many different insects appear without any transitions—like dragonflies. They appear suddenly in the fossil record, and the highly complex systems that enable their aerodynamic abilities have no ancestors in the fossil record. This lack of transitions between species in the fossil record is what would be expected if life was created.

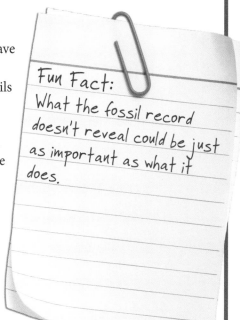

Fun Fact:
What the fossil record doesn't reveal could be just as important as what it does.

Rapid and Catastrophic Burial

Fossils universally provide evidence of rapid burial and even agonizing death. The abundant marine (water-dwelling) invertebrate fossils throughout all of the fossil layers demonstrate extraordinary burial conditions. Think about what happens to a fish when it dies. It either floats to the surface or sinks to the bottom, where it decays and/or is eaten by scavengers. But many fish fossils are so carefully preserved that even their scales and organs are undamaged—there was no time for decay and bacterial action.

Fossils Found at All Levels

The earth is covered with layers of sedimentary rock that were formed from the sediment deposited by enormous water and mudflows. Those continent-covering, water-deposited layers contain countless fossils—including marine creatures at all levels that appear suddenly and fully formed. For example, clams are found in the bottom layer, the top layer, and every layer in between. There are many different varieties of clams, but clams are in every layer and resemble the clams that are still alive today, demonstrating no evolution—just clams! The same could be said for corals, jellyfish, and many other creatures.

From the bottom layers to the top layers, most fossils are marine creatures. The upper levels do have an increasing number of vertebrates, such as fish, amphibians, reptiles, and mammals, but the fossils at the bottom levels are just as complex as any animal today. All fossil types appear suddenly, fully formed, and fully functional without more simple ancestors under them. The fossil record is strong evidence for the sudden appearance of life by creation, followed by rapid burial during a global flood.

Adapted from Morris III, H. M. 2009. *Exploring the Evidence for Creation.* Dallas, TX: Institute for Creation Research.

For more extraordinary evidence, check out The Fossil Record *at the ICR.org store!*

Back to the Bible

"All in whose nostrils was the breath of the spirit of life, all that was on the dry land, died....Only Noah and those who were with him in the ark remained alive."

— Genesis 7:22-23

Read

Genesis 7

Respond

1. List some of the action words the Bible uses to record the Flood account.

   _____
   _____

2. Of the animals that were not on the Ark, which ones died and which ones might have survived the Flood?

   _____
   _____

3. How does the Bible's record line up with the fossil record?

   _____
   _____

4. Why do you think the history recorded in the Bible can be so unpopular?

   _____
   _____

Takeaways

- The Bible details a worldwide flood that caused widespread death and destruction and that clearly explains the fossil record we see today.

- Even with the scientific evidence on your side, you'll discover that believing the great Flood buried the majority of fossils is an unpopular viewpoint, but popularity has nothing to do with truth.

- How can you prepare yourself to share what is true with people who may disagree with you?

Awesome Activities for All Ages

1. Road trip

   As a group: Take a field trip to a local road-cut where rock layers have been exposed during the building of a road. Look for fossils. Often, clam shell fragments can be discovered.

   Discuss why clams do not ordinarily become fossilized today. Research what kinds of animals or processes eat or erode clam shells.

2. Make a fossil in a month

   Create your own fossils using at-home science and cement kits. Or, use locally available mud or soil. Drill holes in the bottom of a five-gallon bucket that has a lid. Sandwich organisms like leaves, insects, or fish between layers of mud. Seal the bucket for a month. Carefully excavate the "fossils" layer-by-layer like a paleontologist, describing the conditions of the remains. How does the number of fossils you find compare to the number of organisms you buried? If there are fewer fossils, why?

3. Museum trip

   As a group, visit the origins section of your local natural history museum.

   Younger students: Identify the different types of fossils and the modern animals they are most like. What similarities do you see between fossils and modern kinds? What differences?

   Older students: Talk through the exhibits based on a biblical worldview. Pick one exhibit and/or description to rewrite based on a creation worldview. How would the new information change the visual presentation of the exhibit?

4. Research

   Older students: Download the PowerPoint file at ICR.org/fossil-record and use the images to present four key features of fossils to the group—features that confirm the fossils were deposited by Noah's Flood or post-Flood calamities in the recent past.

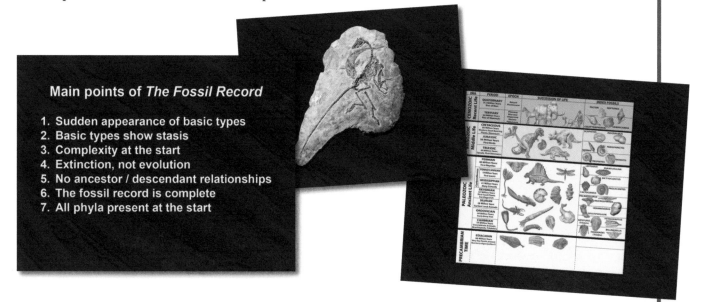

Main points of *The Fossil Record*

1. Sudden appearance of basic types
2. Basic types show stasis
3. Complexity at the start
4. Extinction, not evolution
5. No ancestor / descendant relationships
6. The fossil record is complete
7. All phyla present at the start

5

Flood or Fiction?

Noah's Ark is one of the first Bible stories you may have learned, but it's more than just a story. Today's scientific evidence supports the truth of the Flood as a very real event that permanently changed the geology and climate of planet Earth.

"By the word of God the heavens were of old, and the earth standing out of water and in the water, by which the world that then existed perished, being flooded with water."

— 2 Peter 3:5-6

Bible scholars aren't the only ones who think there was a worldwide flood. Stories of a great flood that wiped out everyone except one small group of people are found in ancient texts and folklore from cultures all over the world. Secular and creation scientists agree that there has been major, catastrophic flooding in Earth's past. If Noah's Flood happened as Genesis describes, what does that reveal about our origins? And could it happen again?

Brainy Buzzwords

Noah's Flood: A Truly Perfect Storm

Use the clues to solve the puzzle below!

Across

4. Mountain that provided great evidence supporting catastrophism and the Flood (3 words)

6. Of or having to do with water

9. Process by which sediments are shifted and moved

11. Theory that Earth's geological features are consequences of a catastrophic event

12. First book of the Bible

13. Post-Flood period of extended cold and freezing (2 words)

15. Righteous man that God used to preserve humans and animals from the Flood

Down

1. "The present is the key to the past."

2. Another name for Earth's sedimentary layers

3. A story that is passed down through generations and may or may not be true

5. The process by which sediments are laid down in a specific area

7. The study of Earth's rocks, sediments, and physical changes

8. A famous natural wonder found in Arizona (2 words)

9. Factual data used to try to make a point

10. Length of time that it rained during Noah's Flood (2 words)

14. Big "box" that God instructed Noah to build

Brainy Buzzwords

Did That Ark Float?

Using the word bank below, fill in the blanks. Some words may be used more than once!

agreement   climate   Flood   past
beliefs   creationists   geological   processes
billions   deposition   geologists   secularists
Canyon   destructive   gradual   short
catastrophe   erosion   key   time
catastrophism   evidence   life   uniformitarianism
changes   evolutionary   opposite

1. Scientists, both _____ and _____, agree that there was major, catastrophic flooding in Earth's past. However, that's where their _____ ends.

2. Scientists have two very different opinions of Noah's _____ based on two different presuppositions (assumptions made beforehand). To better understand both points of view, it helps to understand two really big words that are _____ to our discussion: *uniformitarianism* and *catastrophism*.

3. These are two different foundational _____ that explain why two scientists who look at the same _____ can come back with two different conclusions.

4. _____ is the doctrine that _____ like erosion and deposition that we observe today operated in exactly the same way in Earth's remote geological past. An easier way of remembering this is the phrase "the present is the key to the _____."

5. This concept underlies the belief that our world is _____ of years old. Secular scientists believe that a single layer of geological strata represents a significant amount of _____— even millions of years—of Earth's activity. These secular scientists acknowledge that there have been _____ to the landscape over these millions of years but still believe that the changes have been slow and _____ and happened at a fairly constant rate. Does that sound familiar? That's because if you apply uniformitarian thinking to biology—the study of _____—you get _____ ideas.

6. Creation scientists see the world in the _____ way. They don't assume that processes like _____ and _____ that we see today happened in exactly the *same* ways in the past as they do now. That's because between what we see now and what we would have seen then there's been a world-altering, watery _____ that resulted in our present-day _____ formations.

7. This doctrine of _____ says that Earth-surface features, like the rock layers and erosion in Grand _____, are the consequences of a key catastrophic event: a violent, _____ flood and its aftereffects. Contrary to uniformitarianists, Flood _____ say that the forces that have shaped Earth's landscape and altered its geology and _____ were all caused in a very _____ timeframe by a single, year-long catastrophic event—Noah's _____.

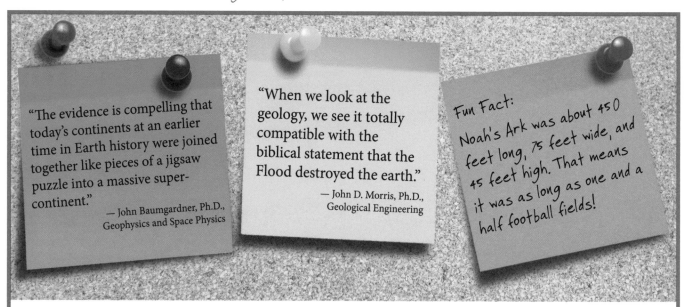

"The evidence is compelling that today's continents at an earlier time in Earth history were joined together like pieces of a jigsaw puzzle into a massive super-continent."

— John Baumgardner, Ph.D., Geophysics and Space Physics

"When we look at the geology, we see it totally compatible with the biblical statement that the Flood destroyed the earth."

— John D. Morris, Ph.D., Geological Engineering

Fun Fact:
Noah's Ark was about 450 feet long, 75 feet wide, and 45 feet high. That means it was as long as one and a half football fields!

Think Tank

1. Describe the two very different opinions that scientists have about the Genesis Flood account.

   _____

   _____

2. What do you get when you apply the uniformitarian viewpoint to biology?

   _____

3. List some common reasons why uniformitarian scientists say the Flood didn't happen.

   _____

   _____

4. According to creationists, how long ago did the Flood take place?

   _____

   _____

5. Why is it inaccurate to imagine the Flood in terms of just a lot of heavy rain? How should we think of it? Give some modern-day examples.

   _____

   _____

6. How do creationists explain how the floodwaters could have covered giant mountains like Mount Everest?

   _____

   _____

7. Where did much of the Flood's water come from?

   _____

   _____

8. How would most scientists describe the organization of our continents in ancient times?

   _____

   _____

9. How does the Mount St. Helens eruption support Noah's Flood?

   _____

   _____

Extraordinary Evidence

What scientific evidence indicates that Noah's Flood was real and that it permanently changed the geology and climate of planet Earth? Why is this important for our view of origins?

Evidence for a Worldwide Catastrophe

Skeptics of creation science often claim that no evidence for the Flood exists. Even though most geologists have abandoned uniformitarianism in favor of a grudging acceptance of catastrophism, they still deny the global, year-long Flood that Scripture describes.

However, strata containing marine fossils provide critical evidence that the ocean once covered the continents—even the highest continental areas. Extremely widespread strata deposits argue for an intercontinental or global flood. Tremendous amounts of water moving very quickly have left scars throughout the earth's major formations. Catastrophic displacements of enormous plates of the earth's crust provided the driving force for the global Flood and produced the deep spaces for the oceans to drain into afterward. The majority of our planet's sedimentary rock appears to have accumulated rapidly by means of a worldwide deluge.

> **Fun Fact:**
> The Greek word used to describe the Flood in 2 Peter is *kataklusmos*, from which we get the English word *cataclysm*.

"Testing" the Past

The best that a scientist can do with past geologic events that were not observed is to evaluate the clues in the rocks and the fossils and try to understand them in the light of present processes or by comparing hydraulic (moving water) forces on a much smaller scale.

Science makes predictions based on hypotheses. This is especially true of historical or forensic science since the scientist was not around to see the actual event take place. The hypothesis that best fits the facts is most likely the accurate picture of what happened. When predictions about a model or theory are not confirmed by the data, science suggests that the hypothesis is incorrect.

Evidence for Rapid Formation

Looking at the Bible's record, we would predict that the geologic results of the Flood would show that the strata were deposited by catastrophic processes operating on a regional scale. But uniformitarian scientists would predict that the rock record would be dominated by results of the slow, gradual geologic processes observed today, operating on a local scale.

However, there is extensive evidence that strata in the geologic record were laid down very quickly, similar to processes observed when Mount St. Helens erupted. The major formations of Earth's crust are sedimentary rock beds formed by rapid erosion, transportation, and deposition by water. There is no global evidence of great lengths of time between these layers or indications that these layers took long periods of time to form.

Consider the Columbia River Basalt Group of lava flows in Washington, Oregon, and Idaho. This series of lava flows was stacked one on top of another in rapid succession and covers an area of some 65,000 square miles, with a volume of about 40,000 cubic miles. Underneath the Columbia River Basalts we find thick layers of water-deposited, fossil-bearing, sedimentary rock, obviously deposited by the Flood itself.

Such large-scale volcanic activity does not match uniformitarian predictions. But it does match the creation-Flood young earth prediction of catastrophic processes operating on a regional scale during and right after the Flood. While neither side directly observed the past, the biblical model is the one that best predicts the evidence. So, from a scientific perspective, it is more likely correct.

Adapted from Morris III, H. M. 2009. *Exploring the Evidence for Creation*. Dallas, TX: Institute for Creation Research.

For more extraordinary evidence, check out The Global Flood *at the ICR.org store!*

Back to the Bible

> "Scoffers will come in the last days...saying, 'Where is the promise of His coming? For since the fathers fell asleep, all things continue as they were from the beginning of creation."
> — 2 Peter 3:3-4

Read

Genesis 6-9 • 2 Peter 3:3-6

Respond

1. What common origins viewpoint does 2 Peter 3:3-6 describe? _____

2. List all of the ways that Peter describes the scoffers. _____

3. What do the scoffers "willfully forget"? _____

4. In the context of the entire chapter, why do you think that Peter specifically mentions the Flood in 2 Peter 3:3-6? _____

5. Do you know anyone who reminds you of the people Peter is talking about in this passage? How could you approach them with the truth about creation and the Flood? _____

6. How might Noah and his experience with the Flood be a picture of what Jesus did for us? _____

7. What was God's covenant with Noah? Does this mean that catastrophe will never strike the earth again? Why or why not? _____

Takeaways

- The Bible says a lot about the Flood—dimensions of the Ark, geological details, and more. But mostly it shows us that we should take the worldwide Flood seriously. The evidence that creation scientists are uncovering indicates that the events described in Genesis were more than a great adventure story—they really happened.

- Sometimes it takes courage to go against popular ideas and stand firm in your faith like Noah did. When we do, we can be certain that the same God that took care of Noah on the Ark is the same God we can trust to provide for us.

Awesome Activities for All Ages

1. Cause a global flood

   Using sand—or mixtures of sand and other sediment—and a clear, empty container, create a replica of the earth's strata. Have students take turns pouring water at different rates to see how drastic waterflow during the Flood—not just rain—would have created worldwide destruction and layered deposits.

2. Mount St. Helens

   Younger Students: Create a picture history of the Mount St. Helens eruption using images printed from the Internet or from magazines.

   Older Students: Research the Mount St. Helens eruption and write a one-page comparison of quotes from secular scientists and creation scientists relating to the event. As a family, talk through the importance of Mount St. Helens to creation science using the research you've done and the collages you've created.

3. Reading time

   As a family, read the Genesis Flood account in Genesis 6-9.

   Younger students: Illustrate a scene based on what you heard from the Bible reading.

   Older students: Write down key details that specifically line up with what the scientific evidence shows.

   As a group: Using the dimensions and descriptions in the Bible, butcher paper, and art materials, draw the Ark to scale. If time permits, add illustrations of Noah's family and a few favorite animals as they would have been grouped to enter the Ark.

4. Visualize Noah's Ark

   As a family: Determine the length of your gait. Obtain a convenient ratio, such as five natural steps are ~15 feet. In a large field, pace off the appropriate number of steps based on the Ark's dimensions, and place one person at each of the Ark's four corners. Take a picture. Does the "Ark" take up as much space as you imagined?

Episode

6

How Old Is Earth?

We can answer the question "How old is Earth?" by turning to science and the Bible. In both cases, faith plays a part.

"For in six days the LORD made the heavens and the earth, the sea, and all that is in them, and rested the seventh day."

— Exodus 20:11

When we ask how old Earth is, we're really asking a history question. What is our planet's history? How long has it been here? How was it formed? Unfortunately, no human being was around to see it happen. The best we can do is look at clues, test them with modern science and technology, and draw conclusions based on the results. What does Genesis say about Earth's age, and how do scientists estimate it?

Brainy Buzzwords

Earth: Young or Old?

Unscramble the letters below to reveal important terms surrounding the age of the earth!

ASSUMPTION	DECAY	LIGHT	TAPEATS
BIBLE	EVIDENCE	MILLIONS	THOUSANDS
CARBON	FAITH	PLANET	URANIUM
CIVILIZATION	FLOOD	PROCESS	VOLCANO
CLOCK	GEOCHRONOLOGY	RADIOACTIVE	
CONSTANT	HISTORY	SCIENTIFIC	
DARKNESS	LAYERS	STRATA	

1. CVNALOO _____
2. DATOHNSSU _____
3. ATSTAR _____
4. USMSPOATIN _____
5. RNOBCA _____
6. CKCLO _____
7. OEADIVIACTR _____
8. NPLTEA _____
9. LTIHG _____
10. CANTTNOS _____
11. CDEYA _____
12. HITAF _____
13. OOLDF _____
14. YELRSA _____
15. NOMISLIL _____
16. DEVIECEN _____
17. NEDSRKAS _____
18. LOTZINCVAIII _____
19. ILEBB _____
20. TYHSROI _____
21. SPSRCOE _____
22. RNAIMUU _____
23. OOOCENOHGRGYL _____
24. STAEATP _____
25. NSEIFCTCII _____

Brainy Buzzwords

Age of Mystery?

Using the word bank below, fill in the blanks. Some words may be used more than once!

age	Earth	Grand	rate	thousands
carbon	estimate	history	rocks	time
clues	faith	hourglass	sand	uniform
conclusions	fast	human	scientists	younger
constant	fossils	millions	see	

1. When we ask how old Earth is, we're really asking a history question. What is our planet's
    _____? Unfortunately, no _____ being was around to _____
    the beginning. The best we can do is look at clues, test them with modern science and technology, and
    draw _____ based on the results.

2. The _____ of Earth is a fundamental question. All scientists work with the same data or "evi-
    dence": the same chemical, biological, and physical _____. The key is how researchers
    interpret the information they get. To find the answers, we turn to both science *and* the Bible. In both
    cases, _____ comes into play.

3. All _____ start with certain assumptions about the past and then use faith in those as-
    sumptions, together with geology, physics, and chemistry, to make certain calculations about Earth's age,
    or, more specifically, its _____. This is called *geochronology*. There are several different
    ways to do this, and we sometimes get different results.

4. The clocks that many scientists use to estimate the age of rocks have things in common. They all assume,
    by faith, a *constant process rate*, like the _____ falling in an hourglass. We assume the
    sand will always fall at a _____ rate. Next, scientists need to have what's called a *closed
    process system*, like the hourglass; nothing can get in there and interfere with the measurements.

5. And finally, scientists have to begin with a *known initial process component*, again, like the sand. When
    we use an _____, we know how much sand we started with, so we know how much
    _____ has passed as it falls.

6. The secular dates for rocks like the ones in _____ Canyon depend on one thing: uni-
    formitarianism. Has everything always happened at a _____ rate? Like the sand falling
    in an hourglass, have processes always happened at a constant speed? Or have they sometimes gone very
    _____?

7. Because of the Mount St. Helens eruption in 1980, we know that sediment layers can form really
    _____. We know that _____-14 is often found in fossils that secular
    scientists have dated as being millions of years old—it should be long gone by now! This implies that the
    _____ (and the sediment-bearing rocks they are found in) aren't millions of years old
    but only _____! We also know that radioactive elements like uranium have not always
    decayed at the same _____.

8. If geologic processes haven't been constant, then that's a huge problem for the uniformitarian outlook.
    If the rate of change in the _____ wasn't constant and if strata didn't form
    slowly over _____ of years, then the assumptions scientists have been using
    to _____ our planet's age aren't reliable. Earth could really be much
    _____ than secular scientists say.

"The Hebrew word for day is *yom,* and it can, perhaps in certain poetic contexts like in the 'day of the Lord'...mean a longer period of time than 24 hours, but not in the context of Genesis 1."

— Jason Lisle, Ph.D., Astrophysics

"Carbon-14 is routinely found in significant levels in fossils that are supposedly tens to hundreds of millions of years old....What this implies is that all fossils are not millions of years old but only thousands."

— John Baumgardner, Ph.D., Geophysics and Space Physics

Fun Fact: Geochronology: Science concerned with the ordering and dating of events in the earth's history, including the age of Earth itself.

Think Tank

1. List some of the common evidences that all scientists use to evaluate Earth's age.
_____
_____

2. What are three assumptions shared by "clocks" scientists use?
_____
_____
_____

3. What is one assumption secular scientists make about the decay rate of uranium to end up with ages of millions of years for Grand Canyon?
_____
_____

4. What problems do fossils containing carbon-14, soft tissue, and DNA create for secular dating?
_____
_____

5. What are two main views about how Grand Canyon formed?
_____
_____

6. What specific Grand Canyon feature supports the reality of Noah's Flood?
_____
_____

7. What do you think is the best piece of evidence you could present to support that the earth and its rock layers did not form over long ages?
_____
_____
_____

8. Why does the age of the earth matter for us today?
_____
_____

Extraordinary Evidence

Understanding the approximate age of the earth is more than a scholarly topic—it's an important issue of faith. Scientific evidence shows why basic assumptions about Earth's age may be flawed and that our planet's ancient past may not be so ancient after all.

All Measurement "Clocks" Depend on Unprovable Assumptions

Any geochronometric calculation (dating of the earth) is based on at least the following assumptions: a constant process rate, a closed process system, and known initial process components. However, not one of these three critical assumptions is provable, or testable, or reasonable, or even possible! Therefore, no geochronometric calculation can possibly be certain, and most of them are probably full of mistakes.

Since the size of the error in the assumptions will vary a great deal from process to process, we can expect to get a wide range of "apparent ages." The book *The Young Earth* (available at ICR.org) explains the calculations necessary to arrive at "origin" dates and lists 76 processes for calculating the age of various key parts of the earth. Interestingly enough, all of them date the earth as much younger than standard evolutionary estimates of billions of years.

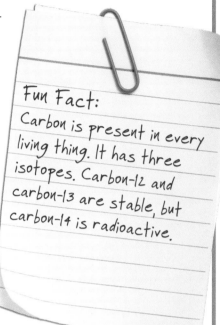

Fun Fact:
Carbon is present in every living thing. It has three isotopes. Carbon-12 and carbon-13 are stable, but carbon-14 is radioactive.

Many Strata Are Too Tightly Bent

In many mountain areas, strata (layers of earth) thousands of feet thick are bent and folded into hairpin shapes. The conventional geologic timescale says these formations were deeply buried and solidified for *hundreds of millions of years* before they were bent. Yet the folding occurred without cracking, with radii so small that the entire formation had to still be wet and unsolidified when the bending occurred. This implies that the folding of these layers occurred less than thousands of years after the sediments were deposited.

Diamonds Have Too Much Carbon-14

Natural diamonds are believed to have formed deep underground in the upper mantle of the earth's crust millions of years ago. Under extreme temperature and pressure, pure carbon changes into the diamond's crystalline form. Rising magma moves the diamond upward.

If the rate that carbon-14 decays has been consistent, current measuring techniques cannot detect any carbon-14 older than 100,000 years. But here is a significant problem for the supposed long ages: natural diamonds contain carbon-14. That means either the decay rate of carbon-14 is not uniform, the diamonds are younger than believed, or both. Carbon-14 in diamonds is evidence that the earth is thousands of years old, not millions.

The Sea Does Not Have Enough Minerals

Every year, more salt enters the ocean from rivers and accumulates. At present rates, seawater is not as salty as it should be if the oceans were ancient. Looking at the present rate the salt content is increasing per year, the current 3.5% salinity of seawater is much too low if this process has been going on for a very long time.

Adapted from Morris III, H. M. 2009. *Exploring the Evidence for Creation*. Dallas, TX: Institute for Creation Research.

For more extraordinary evidence, check out The Young Earth *at the ICR.org store!*

Back to the Bible

"And God saw the light, that it was good; and God divided the light from the darkness. God called the light Day, and the darkness He called Night. So the evening and the morning were the first day."

— Genesis 1:4-5

Read

Genesis 1:4-5 • Exodus 20:11 • Exodus 31:16-17 • 1 Corinthians 14:33

Respond

1. Write down all of the details you observe about the description of creation and what makes a day a "day."
   _____
   _____

2. What clues indicate that the Bible is actually talking about 24-hour days? _____
   _____

3. Why is an understanding of how a day is defined so important to how we read Genesis? _____
   _____
   _____

4. Taking an exhaustive analytical Bible concordance, look up the Hebrew word *yom* and cross-check it with the word "day." How many times is *yom* translated as "day" in the Bible? In the book of Genesis? How many times is it used in Genesis to refer to the creation account? Can you find any use in Genesis of the word "day" (as a translation of *yom*) where it does not make sense if it is interpreted as a literal 24-hour day? _____
   _____
   _____

5. What does 1 Corinthians 14:33 tell us about God? How does this apply to His work of creation and our understanding of origins? _____
   _____

Takeaways

- The Bible describes exactly what a day is when it talks about the light being "divided from" the darkness and when it says that the "evening and the morning" make a day. How we define a day matters because it affects how old we believe the earth is.

- The age of the earth matters because it connects to how everything began. If the Bible is wrong or misleading about time in its very first chapters, where else could it be wrong?

- Scientific evidence supports the Bible and suggests that Earth's age can be accurately counted in thousands, not millions, of years.

Awesome Activities for All Ages

1. Library time

    Go to your local library and check out picture books on Grand Canyon to help facilitate discussion. Or, acquire *The Global Flood, The Young Earth,* or *Footprints in the Ash* from ICR.org, and use selected sections as creation conversation starters.

2. Soil sample project

    Talk through the scientific method as a group. Have students hypothesize about the type of soil layers they think they will find in the sample area and why. Use hand-held core samplers or shovels to sample sediment layers in different areas of your yard. Visit a road-cut where soil layers have been exposed due to the building of a road. Talk about the "history" of that cross-section and what may have caused those layers.

    Younger students: Take turns helping with the sampling. Provide them with worksheets showing predrawn, empty core samplers. Have them color in the core sampler pictures with the colors and depth of layers they see in the "field."

    Older students: Create a graph with a legend to document the data they collect from the core samples. Give students examples of different ways they can construct their graph, but let them choose to represent the data however they wish, as long as it is clear.

    As a family: Discuss and record the conclusions that the students arrive at based on the data they collect from the sample areas. Were their hypotheses correct? Why or why not? Access ICR's article "The Stones Cry Out" at ICR.org and see if it applies to your sample area.

3. Field trip

    Take a field trip to your local arboretum or botanic gardens. Schedule a talk with an expert on how soil and water interact and how the grounds crew handles problems related to types of soil, erosion, and deposition.

    Younger students: Each student will come up with one good question that they would like to ask the expert.

    Older students: Prepare three to five questions that they would like to ask the expert.

4. Date the artifacts

    Visit an antique shop or thrift store to examine old items—or use antiques with known ages from home. Have students select items and try to determine their ages. How accurate were the guesses? What observations proved to be reliable, and what were some things that were misleading? Explore the advantages and disadvantages of age-dating methods that rely on written records versus natural processes like decay, rust and other oxidation reactions, or erosion.

5. The heat problem

    Research the heat problem that planets like Saturn and moons like Io pose to evolutionary time. To illustrate, bake a potato in the oven. Carefully remove the potato and place a thermometer in it. Have students take turns recording the temperature every 10 minutes for an hour and summarize any temperature trend. If Saturn is billions of years old, then why does it still give off heat like a hot potato?

Episode

7

Dinosaurs!

Where do dinosaurs fit into
a Christian view of the world?

"Look now at the behemoth,
which I made along with you."

— Job 40:15

Secular scientists tell us dinosaurs went extinct 66 million years ago, but how does that fit with the history of Adam and Eve and what we are learning about the age of the earth? Did dinosaurs really live and die before man existed? Or could they have walked the earth at the same time as humans?

Brainy Buzzwords

Disappearing Dinos: A History Mystery

Using the word bank below, fill in the blanks. Some words may be used more than once!

66	creatures	Genesis	powerful	structure
225	dating	humans	radioactive	thighbone
Age	design	layer	rocks	world
carbon	dinosaurs	legends	similar	worldwide
catastrophic	evolution	Mary Schweitzer	six	writing
constant	floods	Mesozoic	soft	
creation	fossils	million	stories	

1. We're told that the _____ of the Dinosaurs, part of the _____ Era, began about _____ million years ago—supposedly long before man—and ended in mass extinction supposedly around _____ million years ago.

2. According to _____, God created the earth and man and *all* the living _____ in the _____ days of creation. Creating wonderfully designed _____ would have been no problem for an all-knowing, all-_____ God.

3. Here's an easy way to remember key facts about dinosaurs—the 5 Cs:

   a. *Created*. Dinosaur pelvic _____ is more consistent with _____ than with a slow _____. There's definite evidence of divine _____ in the way those bones fit together.

   b. *Catastrophe*. Everyone agrees that the dinosaurs we find in the rock strata were killed off suddenly by some great and _____ event. And we find dinosaurs in layer upon _____ of _____ deposited by water on every continent! Secular scientists believe these layers and the _____ found in them were caused by local _____ and other small catastrophes with _____s of years in between. But could it have been a year-long, _____ flood?

   c. *Carbon*. _____-dating only works when there is organic matter present and when the samples are less than 100,000 years old.

   d. *Collagen*. That's _____ tissue, but remember that fossils are supposed to be _____. There shouldn't be any organic material in them. But in 2004, Dr. _____ _____ found soft tissue in a tyrannosaur _____ that had been thought to be about 70 _____ years old.

   e. *Clashes*. Did _____ have contact with dinosaurs? People have been writing about them for as long as humans have been _____. We find these fantastic creatures in _____ from cultures around the _____. Maybe people have actually encountered dinosaurs—that's why these _____ are so _____, no matter where you go.

Brainy Buzzwords

Dino Hunt

See how quickly you can find the names of these dinosaurs unearthed at Dinosaur National Monument in the puzzle below. Words may be spelled vertically, horizontally, diagonally, or backward.

ABYDOSAURUS	BAROSAURUS	DIPLODOCUS
ALLOSAURUS	CAMARASAURUS	DRYOSAURUS
APATOSAURUS	CAMPTOSAURUS	STEGOSAURUS

U C S U C U A L A R B D S T
A O O P S S A A U O U I R A
S D O U U U G S A R S P O O
U T R U O A U A O U S L A L
R U E Y S S U Y R U S O A U
U G R G O O A U R R U D U S
A P A T O S A U R U S O P S
S U R U A S A R A M A C C R
O B A R O S A U R U S U B S
T R U D O A L U R A A S C P
P U Y L S U M D R U R O A A
M B L R O C R B D U S O A R
A A R U S A S D R U S S A I
C O A S R A A U A A A O G S

"Some dinosaur fossils still contain original proteins that never turned into minerals, and lab experiments clearly show that even the most resilient proteins can't last millions of years."

— Brian Thomas, M.S., Biotechnology

"Based on the dinosaur graveyards—based on the fact that we see very different animals like dinosaurs and small snails and clams all mixed together—… [Dinosaur National Monument] was a very catastrophic deposit."

— John Whitmore, Ph.D., Biology

Fun Fact:
Did you know that most dinosaurs were little—about the size of a modern dog?

Think Tank

1. What different ideas do secular and creation scientists have about when dinosaurs lived? _____
   _____
   _____

2. What's the most popular theory about dinosaur extinction? _____
   _____
   _____

3. During fossilization, what happens to a dead organism after its soft tissues rot away? Why is it so important for paleontologists to spot a fossil and retrieve it quickly once it is exposed? _____
   _____
   _____

4. What aspects of dinosaur anatomy and fossil evidence suggest that dinosaurs were created as an entirely different type of reptile—not as ancestors of modern reptiles? _____
   _____
   _____

5. What evidence indicates that the deposits in the Morrison Formation resulted from a catastrophe? _____
   _____
   _____

6. What newer evidence has raised serious questions about the real ages of fossils? _____
   _____
   _____

7. Do you think dinosaurs lived at the same time as humans? Why or why not? _____
   _____
   _____

8. What is the strongest evidence you can give from science and the Bible to explain the creation perspective on dinosaurs' history to someone who has never heard it before? _____
   _____
   _____

Extraordinary Evidence

If we believe the Bible is true, then dinosaurs were created with the other creatures and humans. So, what happened during the great Flood? Did dinosaurs survive on Noah's Ark too?

Dinosaurs on the Ark?

The years leading up to the worldwide Flood judgment were no doubt filled with animal violence as well as man's sin. The only solution was their destruction (Genesis 6:11-13). By this time, the land-dwelling bird, mammal, and reptile kinds had somehow been spoiled—morphed into monsters that, although they still had their basic created forms, became ruined castoffs from their well-behaved original ancestors.

But the Lord did bring some dinosaurs to Noah, presumably to a staging ground from which Noah and his family brought them into the Ark at just the right time (Genesis 7:14-15).

This is a crazy suggestion to those who haven't researched how possible it really was, but the dinosaurs could easily have been housed on board. Here are some answers to some common questions about dinosaurs on the Ark.

Fun Fact:
The largest dinosaurs were sauropods. They could weigh as much as 55 tons, and some of them were as long as half of a football field!

Q How could Noah have squeezed the thousands of different dinosaur species into the Ark along with all those other animals?

A Noah's family did not bring each species but two of each kind. Paleontologists make careers out of inventing species names, but there were really only about 60 different basic dinosaur kinds. With no problem, 120 dinosaurs averaging the size of a medium-size dog would have occupied a small corner of the huge ship.

Q How could Noah have fit on board enough live animals to feed all those hungry dinosaurs for a whole year?

A Noah could have fed the dinosaurs Genesis 1 vegetarian diets. He may even have known which plant products they preferred before the Fall since Noah's father, Lamech, might have talked with Adam. Also, reptiles are famous for fasting. Dinos probably ate less than the mammals or birds on board!

Q How could Noah have handled and cared for such terrible toothy tyrants?

A It wasn't until after the Flood that God gave animals, including dinosaurs, a fear of man (Genesis 9:2). Perhaps this made their management much easier during the Flood. If not, we can be sure that Noah's family was as clever as modern humans who have successfully corralled virtually every land creature at one time or another.

Q How would large dinosaurs like *Diplodocus* have fit onto any of the Ark's three decks?

A The largest dinosaur egg is about the size of a football, so even the big-bodied behemoths began small. God probably brought Noah young (and therefore small) sauropods.

Q What happened to the dinosaurs not on the Ark?

A They, along with all other land-dwelling, air-breathing creatures, drowned in the Flood or were suffocated by mud.

Adapted from Thomas, B. 2013. *Dinosaurs and the Bible*. Dallas, TX: Institute for Creation Research, 14-16.
For more extraordinary evidence, check out Dinosaurs and the Bible *at the ICR.org store!*

Back to the Bible

"Look now at the behemoth, which I made along with you; He eats grass like an ox. See now, his strength is in his hips, and his power is in his stomach muscles. He moves his tail like a cedar; the sinews of his thighs are tightly knit."

— Job 40:15-17

Read

Job 40:15-17 • Romans 5:12 • 2 Peter 3:13 • Revelation 21:4

Respond

1. What does Job 40 indicate about when dinosaurs lived?_____
_____

2. What comparisons can you find between the Job 40 behemoth and dinosaurs?
_____
_____

3. What does Romans 5:12 tell us about the origin of death, and how does this connect to ideas about what caused the dinosaurs' extinction? _____
_____

4. What hope do Christians have as death and extinction continue and our world continues to change?
_____
_____

5. What will the new heavens and the new earth be like? _____
_____

Takeaways

- Evolutionists believe dinosaurs prove that the earth is hundreds of millions of years old. But according to Genesis, God created the earth, man, and all the living creatures in the six days of creation.

- Man brought sin and death into the world, and this ultimately led to the extinction of dinosaurs.

- Christians can look forward to eternity in heaven where death no longer exists.

- The same evidence—dinosaurs, fossils, soft tissue, and bone cells—analyzed and tested with the same scientific rigor yields different interpretations based on the worldview of the person interpreting the data. Yet, the scientific evidence conforms to the Bible.

- God's Word gives us insight into the creation of dinosaurs, their burial in a worldwide flood, and their contact with humans after the Flood.

Awesome Activities for All Ages

1. **Museum trip**

   Take a family field trip to view the fossil displays at a natural science museum. Select a few of the exhibits' plaques or fact sheets to analyze, using these critical-thinking questions: 1) How do they know that? and 2) Were eyewitnesses there to verify these facts? Talk about the differences between scientifically verifiable facts and speculative facts, and compile a list of each for the fossil displays. How do the scientific facts fit with creation and the Flood? How can Christians respond to the facts differently in light of 2 Peter 3?

2. **Favorite dinosaurs**

   Younger students: Create a dinosaur collage and include favorite facts about dinos somewhere on the page.

   Older students: Research a favorite dinosaur, draw its picture, label its special features, and write down five main facts about it.

3. **Reading time**

   As a family: Have a group story time and read through some of the eyewitness accounts and legends about dragons.

   Younger students: Talk about where each legend originated. How are the stories similar? How are they different? What do the similarities between stories from different people, different times, and different places hint about dragons?

   Older students: Further research dragon legends, for example, the writings of Marco Polo and Alexander the Great. Create a chart comparing and contrasting these legends, and be sure to include facts from the biblical account in Job. Use the writing prompt "Were Dragons Real?" to create a summary of your findings and conclusions.

3. **Dinos on the Ark**

   As a group, study Scripture's Flood account in Genesis, listing the main features of those creatures that boarded Noah's Ark and the verse reference for each. You should find that they were land-dwelling and had nostrils. Examine dinosaur fossils or their pictures to see if they would have met the Ark's qualifications.

4. **Dino-birds?**

   Evolutionists imagine that dinosaurs evolved into birds, even though reptiles have bellows lungs (where air enters and exits the top of the lungs) and birds have flow-through lungs (where air enters the top and exits the bottom). Illustrate the difficulties with transforming one into the other using simple models. Let a soda straw (or other tubing) that is bent into a U shape represent flow-through design, and use a straw attached to a balloon to represent a bellows design. Then try to reorganize the bellows design into the flow-through design without making any leaks—it's tough to breathe with leaky lungs and tough to live without breathing. What does this tell us about alleged dinosaur evolution?

8

The Ice Age

Most scientists agree that an ice age was the last major geologic event to happen on this planet. But differences of opinion exist on the number of ice ages, when they happened, and how long they lasted.

"So God blessed Noah and his sons, and said to them: 'Be fruitful and multiply, and fill the earth.'"

— Genesis 9:1

Most of us have been taught that there were many ice ages that profoundly influenced the earth's climate, caused mass extinctions, and even altered the way civilization developed. But when it happened and why it happened remain points of conflict among scientists. Evidence of at least one ice age is abundant. But, were there more? Did they last hundreds, thousands, or even millions of years? What caused them, and how does this relate to Noah's Flood?

Brainy Buzzwords

Unpacking the Layers

Match these "ice-related" terms to their definitions below.

1. ____ Aerosols
2. ____ Debris
3. ____ Glacial moraine
4. ____ Glacier
5. ____ Ice Age
6. ____ Ice cores
7. ____ Ice crystal
8. ____ Ice sheet
9. ____ Iceberg
10. ____ Mt. Pinatubo

a. A regular arrangement of frozen water molecules

b. Massive body of dense ice that is constantly moving under its own weight

c. Samples scientists get by drilling deep into polar and glacier ice so they can analyze its chemicals and layers

d. Erupted in 1991 and released a huge amount of aerosols, supporting the theory that the volcanic activity during Noah's Flood could have caused the Ice Age

e. Debris field with boulders, rocks, and dirt that indicates the path the glacier left behind as it moved

f. Disconnected pieces of rock

g. A time after the Flood when some areas in which people live today were covered by giant sheets of ice

h. Tiny, solid particles in liquid droplets that are ejected into the sky by volcanic eruptions and reflect the sun's rays back into space

i. Floating glacier

j. Flat-topped ice body with very broad coverage, also known as a "continental glacier"

Brainy Buzzwords

The Ice Age: Mystery, Madness, or Matter of Fact?

See how quickly you can find all of these words hidden in the puzzle below! Words may be spelled vertically, horizontally, diagonally, or backward.

AEROSOLS

ALASKA

ANTARCTICA

ASTRONOMICAL THEORY

CONTINENTS

CORE

CRYSTALS

DEBRIS

EARTHQUAKE

EVAPORATION

FLOW MODEL

GLACIER

GREENLAND

ICE AGE

LAND BRIDGE

LAYERS

MATANUSKA

MELTING

MORAINE

MOUNT SAINT HELENS

MYSTERY

NOAH'S FLOOD

PINATUBO

TIME

VOLCANO

```
L T O O D D T A U G M L T N E K I L
O R D I I U B O A E R O S O L S K T
N A S T O O S L L M N E N R T I O A
S V R O N T A T U O Y E E E A R T I
N R O A O L I A E R R I L N L I E A
M A T L A N D B R I D G E S L T A R
L O O Y G E A E K A U Q H T R A E E
M S E O B V G C L L S E T N G A N H
Y R E R L A R E L E S E N E O K L D
S A I O E P D A M O R A I N E S S T
T S A C E O R A L O V L A I T U L P
E I I N M R E I C A L G S T S N A I
R E M W O A C I T C R A T N A A T N
Y R O E H T L A C I M O N O R T S A
L L C C Y I T A K R C R U C C A Y T
F O R E N O A H S F L O O D A M R U
L E O O E N O O I K M B M M R T C B
U C I C R E L N O L A S I L Q I N O
```

"The Ice Age would not have been equally severe everywhere....At lower latitudes, you would have had some areas that would have been very lush."

— Jake Hebert, Ph.D., Physics

"The heating of the ocean, we believe, came from magma coming from the mantle up through the plates in the ocean....That would have produced tremendous evaporation...and...snow and ice on the polar regions and on mountaintops."

— Larry Vardiman, Ph.D., Atmospheric Science

Fun Fact:
Crater Glacier on Mount St. Helens is already over 300 feet thick, even though it's only been forming since the 1980 eruption!

Think Tank

1. What evidence do we have for an ice age? _____
_____
_____

2. Compare the uniformitarian and creationist views:
   a. How many ice ages were there? _____
   b. How long did the Ice Age(s) last? _____
   c. How many years ago did the Ice Age(s) happen? _____

3. What do scientists study to arrive at their theories about the Ice Age? _____
_____
_____

4. What are some of the problems with how uniformitarians measure the age of ice—specifically involving ice cores? _____
_____

5. Do colder winters create an ice age? Why or why not? _____
_____
_____

6. What does it really take to cause an ice age? Clue: HEAT. _____
_____
_____

7. What evidence indicates Noah's Flood might have caused the Ice Age? What modern-day catastrophes support this idea? _____
_____
_____

8. What does the creation model say about how humans survived the Ice Age? _____
_____
_____

Extraordinary Evidence

The prevailing view is that many ice ages took place, caused by low-energy processes occurring slowly over millions of years. The creationist view says only one ice age happened, caused by very high-energy processes occurring quickly, and that it lasted for only a few hundred years. What does the evidence reveal?

It's easy to think that colder winters are the key to producing an ice age, but there's more to it than that. Extremely cold temperatures generally mean less, not more, snowfall because extremely cold air does not have as much moisture.[1] Also, some places on Earth today are very cold in the winter, but warm summers melt the winter snow before glaciers can form.[2] An ice age needs cold summers and much more snowfall, and the conditions must continue over many years. In that way, snow and ice can build up year after year.

The Genesis Flood provides these conditions. Extensive, dramatic volcanism would have occurred during the Flood as a consequence of the breaking up of the "fountains of the great deep" and the resulting tectonic activity (movements in Earth's crust).[3] The geologic record contains plenty of evidence for such catastrophic volcanism on a continental scale, although evolutionary scientists incorrectly assign ages of millions of years to these formations.

Basaltic lava flows during the Flood were hundreds—and even thousands—of cubic kilometers in volume.[4,5] Large amounts of lava and hot water would have entered the ocean, causing the water during and after the Flood to have been much warmer than today.[6,7] Flood currents and Earth's movements would have mixed the water so that, after the Flood, the oceans would have been very uniform in temperature, which is unlike today's varied ocean temperatures. More evaporation would have occurred, particularly at the mid and high latitudes, as a result of a higher average ocean surface temperature. This would have provided the additional atmospheric moisture needed for greater snowfall.

Due to the extensive volcanism that occurred more frequently during and after the Flood, the cooler summers needed to keep the winter snow from melting would have been possible. Explosive volcanic eruptions would have ejected large amounts of aerosols (tiny particles) into the stratosphere (region of the upper atmosphere). Even today, aerosols from explosive volcanic eruptions remain suspended in the atmosphere for a number of years, so the same would have been true after the Flood. These aerosols would have reflected a great deal of sunlight back to space, resulting in the cooler summers needed for snow to accumulate. Modern-day volcanic events have shown that volcanic aerosols can cause such cooling.[8]

As the earth slowly regained its balance after the Flood, leftover volcanism would have continued to randomly shoot aerosols into the stratosphere for many years, keeping summers cool enough to prevent the ice from melting. Also, because water has a high heat capacity, it releases heat slowly. So, it would have taken a long time for the oceans to cool to their present average surface temperature.

Meteorologist Michael Oard used "heat budget" equations to estimate the amount of time for the oceans to cool to their present average temperature. Although there are considerable uncertainties in the calculation, he estimated that the post-Flood Ice Age lasted for about 700 years, allowing 500 years for the glaciers to reach their maximum extent and another 200 years for the glaciers to recede.[9] Since the Flood occurred around 2300 B.C., this would mean that the post-Flood Ice Age could have possibly lasted until about 1600 B.C.[10] It may not be a coincidence that the book of Job, believed by conservative scholars to have been written around 2000 B.C., has more references to snow and ice than any other book of the Bible.[11,12]

> **Fun Fact:**
> Did you know that extremely cold temperatures usually result in less, not more, snowfall? Cold air has less moisture. Less moisture means less snow.

Adapted from Hebert, J. 2013. Was There an Ice Age? In *Creation Basics & Beyond*. Dallas, TX: Institute for Creation Research, 239-242. *Endnotes included in Answer Key.*

For more extraordinary evidence, check out The Ice Age and the Flood *and* The Global Flood *at the ICR.org store.*

Back to the Bible

> "I will never again curse the ground for man's sake, although the imagination of man's heart is evil from his youth; nor will I again destroy every living thing as I have done."
>
> — Genesis 8:21

Read

Genesis 8:21 • Genesis 9:1 • Genesis 9:13, 8-17

Respond

1. What did God promise after the Flood? _____
   _____

2. What sign did He give, and what does it represent? _____
   _____
   _____

3. How does the theory of land bridges forming after the Flood fit in with the command God gave Noah and his sons after the Flood? _____
   _____
   _____

4. Based on these post-Flood events, what can we know about God? How should this affect our view of who He is? _____
   _____

Takeaways

- Strong evidence indicates that Noah's Flood created conditions that caused the Ice Age.

- The concept that the Ice Age may not have been as unbearable as we've been told supports the fact that God chose Noah and his family to repopulate the earth.

- By letting Noah and his family live to repopulate the earth and promising to never again destroy the earth with a flood, God showed grace to mankind and gave humanity a second chance.

Awesome Activities for All Ages

1. ## Kitchen experiment

   As a group, experiment with illustrating the Ice Age's weather using a stovetop. Using oven mitts, hold a large square of plastic wrap or a clear lid at a safe distance above a pan of heating water. Try to angle the plastic so that water condensing on its lower surface runs off to the side, and then try to catch that runoff in a plate or bowl placed right next to the heating pot. If the water in the pot represents oceans, the lid represents the atmosphere, and the bowl catching the runoff represents continents, discuss how the heated water affects precipitation in the form of rain on the continents. How would these conditions ultimately create an ice age climate?

2. ## Arctic architecture

   Have each student research a different type of ice formation or a different arctic area—for example, an iceberg or glacier, Antarctica, or Greenland, etc. Have everyone present their findings to the rest of the group.

3. ## Noah and the Ice Age

   Illustrate a scene from any part of the post-Flood story, taking into account what you've learned about the actual climatic conditions when Noah and his family left the Ark. Talk through the details of God's covenant with humans after the Flood. How did the covenant connect to life on Earth during the Ice Age?

   Younger students: Draw pictures and/or cut and paste photographs from magazines to illustrate details of the Ice Age to add to the chart created by older students (below).

   Older students: Create a chart contrasting secular views of the Ice Age with creationist views.

4. ## Ice Age critters

   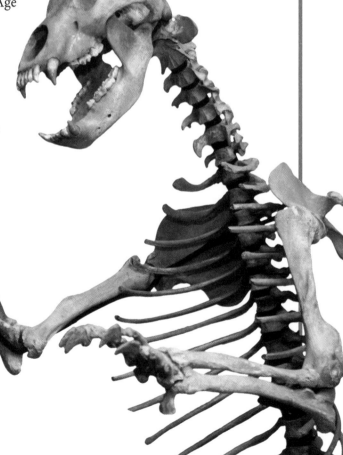

   List several iconic Ice Age animals on a whiteboard or chalkboard. As a family, hypothesize as to whether each kind went extinct or if the animals we have today are just a variation of that kind. For example, cave bears looked much like grizzly bears, so they were most likely a variation within the bear kind. Although the cave variety did go extinct sometime after the Ice Age, bears are not extinct from the world today. Considering the history of encounters between humans and wild, threatening animals, use resources like *The Ice Age and the Flood* and articles from ICR.org to discuss what factors may have led to extinctions of varieties within animal kinds.

English
Pilipino
Svenskt
Kiswahili
Deutsch
български
Türkçe
Việt
Hrvatski
ελληνικά
српски
Italiano
Nederlands
Magyar
русский
ROMÂNĂ
Français
Español
Português

9

Episode

Rise of Civilization

There are over seven billion of us on this planet, living in 200 nations, speaking 6,000 languages. What does the Bible say about human origins and how all of this diversity came about?

"Now the sons of Noah who went out of the ark were Shem, Ham, and Japheth....and from these the whole earth was populated."
— Genesis 9:18-19

The Bible says we are each descended from Noah and his three sons. But is that really possible—seven billion humans descending from the family of one man? Think of all the people who have lived and died, all the countries, all the cultures, and all the civilizations that have existed. Did these really come from a single family? Secular and creation scientists offer different answers about our origins and our development. How did humans come to spread across the planet, speaking different languages and living different lives?

Brainy Buzzwords

The Human Family Tree

Use the clues to solve the puzzle below.

Across

3. Continent secular scientists believe our "common ancestor" came from
4. Birthplace of Abraham
6. Number of major language groups in the world
7. Man responsible for building the Ark
9. Time in history when secular scientists believe man became more advanced and started using written language (3 words)
11. Modern term that focuses more on peoples' differences than their God-given similarities and that has contributed to creating a very negative environment in many cultures
13. One of Noah's three sons whose descendants populated Africa and Asia
14. One of Noah's three sons whose descendants settled in present-day Europe
15. First woman created by God

Down

1. Man who wrote a book illustrating what he thought were physical similarities and differences between humans and apes
2. Principle in genetics that suggests the enforced segregation of mankind into small inbreeding tribal units would generate a rapid development of distinct physical characteristics associated with each tribe (2 words)
3. Continent where the first so-called transitional human fossil was found
5. Place where nations scattered (3 words)
8. First anatomically modern human, according to secular science (2 words)
9. Book where we can find the shared knowledge base of all people groups before they split up
10. One of Noah's three sons whose descendants settled in the Middle East
12. First man created by God

Brainy Buzzwords

Answers from Archaeology

Using the word bank below, fill in the blanks, and learn about the incredible discoveries that support the Bible's record of ancient civilizations. Some words may be used more than once!

150	Babylon	Ebla	mythical
1800	Baghdad	cuneiform	ruins
4,000	Bible	evidence	Tablets
Abraham	Chaldeans	fragments	thrived
archaeologists	cultures	Gomorrah	

1. In the mid-_____s, expeditions by John G. Taylor near the Iraqi city of _____ excavated the famous Ziggurat of Ur. Among the _____, Taylor found _____ cylinders that identified the site by its biblical name "Ur of the _____"—the birthplace of _____. Until that time, Ur had been considered a _____ city, but now there is no denying that the historical _____ confirmed what was written in the _____.

2. Another groundbreaking discovery happened in 1974 when an Italian archaeologist uncovered the _____ of Ebla in Tell Mardikh, an ancient city in modern Syria. These clay tablets were covered with writings in ancient Sumerian, as well as in a local language of _____. There were 1,800 complete tablets and about 4,700 _____ determined to date from between 2500 and 2250 B.C. The tablets likewise make reference to people and places we find in the _____, like Sodom and _____.

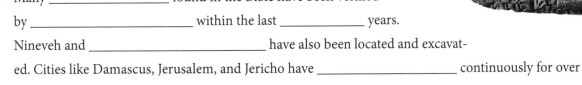

3. Many _____ found in the Bible have been verified by _____ within the last _____ years. Nineveh and _____ have also been located and excavated. Cities like Damascus, Jerusalem, and Jericho have _____ continuously for over _____ years.

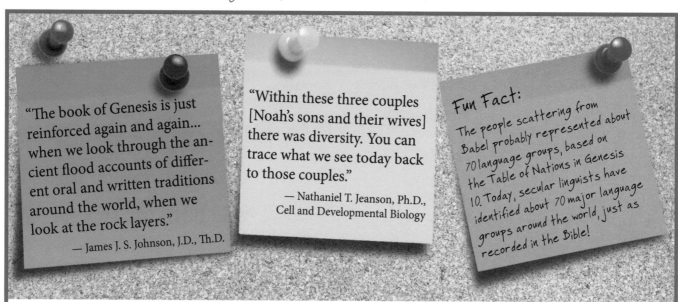

"The book of Genesis is just reinforced again and again... when we look through the ancient flood accounts of different oral and written traditions around the world, when we look at the rock layers."

— James J. S. Johnson, J.D., Th.D.

"Within these three couples [Noah's sons and their wives] there was diversity. You can trace what we see today back to those couples."

— Nathaniel T. Jeanson, Ph.D., Cell and Developmental Biology

Fun Fact:
The people scattering from Babel probably represented about 70 language groups, based on the Table of Nations in Genesis 10. Today, secular linguists have identified about 70 major language groups around the world, just as recorded in the Bible!

Think Tank

1. Who was the first person to apply evolution to people, and how did he do this? _____ _____

2. How does the secular perspective explain the details of human evolution? _____ _____ _____

3. How do secular scientists describe the male and female progenitors of the human race? How is this different from the Bible's account of Adam and Eve? _____ _____

4. Secularists claim humans and apes have common ancestors from Africa. How do they explain humans spreading across the continents and forming different races? _____ _____ _____

5. What, supposedly, was the "Great Leap Forward"? _____ _____

6. List some evidence that has been found supporting the Bible as an accurate historical record. What does this indicate about how we should interpret human origins theories? _____ _____ _____

7. How do biblical creationists explain the origin of different languages and the reason why humans spread across the continents? _____ _____

8. How do biblical creationists explain the physical diversity in humans? _____ _____ _____

9. Where does the emphasis on differences within the human race come from? How has this become a negative thing in our world today? _____ _____ _____

Extraordinary Evidence

Secularists and creationists disagree about what caused humans to populate the earth and diversify within those populations. The Bible gives clear and believable reasons for why people spread out across the continents and for their resulting differences in culture and physical appearance.

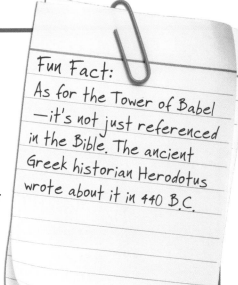

Fun Fact: As for the Tower of Babel —it's not just referenced in the Bible. The ancient Greek historian Herodotus wrote about it in 440 B.C.

The Origin of People Groups

We will never correctly comprehend human origins, migrations, genetics, or languages without considering the Tower of Babel. "From there the LORD scattered them abroad over the face of all the earth" (Genesis 11:9). The events at Babel give us the key to understanding the origin of modern nations and peoples. We are descended from those who were confused and scattered at Babel after the Flood. Babel caused the breakup of the languages and the dispersion of families into all parts of the world.

In the Table of Nations (Genesis 10), we discover a documentation of 70 nations/family groups migrating to fill the earth after Babel. Not surprisingly, linguists have found that the number of separate language groups is basically the same as the 70 listed in Scripture. Genesis 13–50 also mentions locations, towns, and cities that have been verified through the centuries by archaeology, further confirming these basic details and identifying major locations and cultures.

Since the scattering at Babel we have seen only variation within the created kind of people. If this is true, then there are no separate races but only one race—humans (Acts 17:26). Creationists would call the different clusters of people we see throughout the world not "races" but "people groups." We are all humans but quite variable in function and form.

One creation scientist has called this the law of conservation of genetic variability. The human genome is composed of at least six billion nucleotides (the functional units of DNA). Evolutionist Francisco Ayala has said the human genome is 6.7 percent heterozygous (different alleles at a specific gene location) for a variety of the genes.[1] Translated, this means that of every hundred genes, six or seven pairs of genes for a given trait differ, for example, as in the traits of attached or unattached earlobes or the ability to roll the tongue. So, a human couple with this kind of variety can—according to Ayala—produce 10 to the 2,017th power of children that would be unique before producing an identical twin. How big is that number? Physicists estimate there are "only" 10 to the 80th power atoms in the universe. God has created us with an amazing potential for variation!

Take skin color, for example. We all have the same pigments or skin-coloring agents—just different shades or combinations of them. This is due to cells called melanocytes located in the lower epidermis (skin) that produce melanin (dark pigment) granules. How long would it take to get the skin color variation we see in people today? The answer is—a single generation.

Geneticists think it's possible that six genes (DNA) control the type and amount of melanin formed (melanin also contributes to our different eye colors). Although Scripture doesn't say, basic genetics indicates the skin color of Adam and Eve was most likely a middle-brown shade, which can be written as a series of six letters, with each letter representing one allele (AaBbCc). Using a Punnett Square, it can be shown that each parent having these six alleles (copies of a gene) could produce offspring from very dark (AABBCC) to very light (aabbcc) in just one generation due to gene segregation. As people break up into isolated groups, some groups would develop limited variability—only dark (many parts of Africa), only medium (such as in Japan, China, and Polynesia), or only light (much of the Scandinavian population). This variation of skin color—as well as variation in height and all other human function and form—has been built into humans by God, starting with our first parents.

Adapted from Sherwin, F. 2013. Cain, His Wife, and the Origin of Races. In *Creation Basics & Beyond*. Dallas, TX: Institute for Creation Research, 167-171. *Endnotes included in Answer Key.*

For more extraordinary evidence, check out The Genesis Record *and* Guide to Creation Basics *at the ICR.org store!*

Back to the Bible

"He has made from one blood every nation of men to dwell on all the face of the earth, and has determined their preappointed times and the boundaries of their dwellings."

— Acts 17:26

Read

Genesis 9:18-19 • Genesis 10:5, 32 • Genesis 11:1-9 • Psalm 139:14 • Acts 17:26

Respond

1. What does the Bible say about man's origin and God's role in our lives here on Earth?

   _____

   _____

2. What was the ultimate cause of the events at the Tower of Babel? _____

   _____

3. From whom does the Bible say everyone today descended? What facts outside of the Bible can give us confidence to believe this? What results do we find when we use a realistic growth rate and trace the population growth from Noah up through today? _____

   _____

   _____

4. Have you experienced or seen others experience judgment or negative treatment because of their physical appearance or their culture—how they live? Based on what you know the Bible says about our Creator, our origins, and our worth, how should you view that kind of prejudice? _____

   _____

   _____

Takeaways

- Understanding the scientific evidence that supports the biblical account builds confidence in our faith.

- God saved Noah and also scattered people across the earth because He has a plan for mankind.

- God has a plan for all of us—and in it all, He has given us ultimate worth by creating us in His image and sending His Son to die to save us.

- Race is a man-made idea—not something that God instilled. He created everyone unique but with equal value.

Awesome Activities for All Ages

1. Similar but different

    Have each student pick a different ethnicity to research and present in a creative way—use props, costumes, ethnic food sampling, etc.

2. Babbling at the tower

    As a family, simulate what happened at the Tower of Babel by allowing each student only to speak to the others using his or her "cue card"—each cue card will have a different made-up language on it. For example, one student's card might say they can only talk using words that start with the letter "b." Talk about the results of God mixing up languages at the Tower of Babel. Why were the languages mixed? What can you learn from the consequences of defying God? Where can you find grace in the story of Babel?

3. Picture me

    Have each student draw a self-portrait.

    Younger students: Trace an outline of their body on butcher paper, and have them color and decorate it using their favorite art mediums.

    Older students: Draw a realistic self-portrait based on a recent, favorite photograph.

    As a family: Talk about how even within families God has created beautiful variety for a purpose! Discuss the different talents and abilities of each student.

4. Uniquely created

    Younger students: List the ways that God has made you unique. Make a second list of things you can be thankful for because of your special characteristics. What truth can you turn to when you feel like you are less than someone else because of how you look, where you live, or other outward comparisons (Psalm 139)?

    Older students: Write a one-page essay using Scripture to discuss how *not* attributing unique creation to God affects our perceived worth as humans. Cite examples, including at least one from the 20th century and one from current events.

    As a family: Memorize Psalm 139:14.

5. Map it out

    As a group, identify the modern locations below on a world map or globe—pay close attention to what they were called in ancient times. Then, read Genesis 10 and fill in the rest of the chart with the verses that mention leaders with names that sound similar either to a location's modern or ancient name. How do these naming similarities reflect the Bible's accuracy?

Modern Place Name	Alternative / Ancient Place Name	Extinct Culture?	Genesis 10 Verse	Genesis 10 Leader Name
Egypt	Mizr	N		
Assyria	Asshur	Y		
Hebrew (Israel)	Eber	N		
Ethiopia (approx.)	Cush	N		
Birs Nimrud	Tower of Babel	Y		
Palestine	Philistia	N		
Wales	Cambria (Cymru)	N		
Greece	Ionia	N		
Dardanelles	Dardania	N		
Tblisi, Georgia	Tiflis	N		
Tobolsk, Russia	N/A	N		

Episode

10

Origin of the Universe

How did our universe come into being, and how long has it been here?

"The day is Yours, the night also is Yours; You have prepared the light and the sun."

— Psalm 74:16

Science deals with the observable present. What happened in the past is not something we can test scientifically. So, we have to take what we know and work backward to the birth of the universe—at the instant of creation— to understand what happened in the beginning.

Brainy Buzzwords

Lots of Laws

Match each term to its definition.

1. _____ The Law of Increasing Entropy

2. _____ The Law of Cause and Effect

3. _____ Sir Isaac Newton

4. _____ Potential energy

5. _____ Kinetic energy

6. _____ First Law of Thermodynamics

7. _____ George LeMaître

8. _____ Edwin Hubble

9. _____ Cosmic Microwave Background Radiation (CMB)

10. _____ Big Bang

11. _____ Planck satellite

12. _____ Blue stars

13. _____ Spiral galaxies

14. _____ Cosmic inflation

a. His ideas were the beginning of modern physics.

b. Everything is in gradual decay; energy tends to go from a useful form to a useless form.

c. Energy in motion

d. Radiation that Big Bang theorists believe is left over from a time around 400,000 years after the Big Bang

e. Everything with a beginning had a cause

f. Energy waiting to be used

g. These would be so twisted we couldn't recognize them if they were really billions of years old.

h. American scientist who observed that galaxies seemed to be moving away from each other

i. Burn so brightly that they should have burned out long ago if the universe is actually billions of years old

j. Idea that when the universe was supposedly expanding it sped up and then slowed down—used to explain problems secularists are finding with the CMB

k. Catholic priest who theorized that everything started from the explosion of a "primeval atom"

l. Theory that the universe came into existence over 13 billion years ago with a massive explosion

m. Energy cannot be created or destroyed, but can be converted to another form.

n. Launched by NASA in 2009 to study microwave background radiation

Brainy Buzzwords

Space Scramble

Unscramble the letters below to reveal the names of things we can find in space.

ASTEROID   GALACTIC DISK   PLANET
BLACK HOLE   METEOR   RED DWARF
COMET   MICROWAVES   SOLAR ECLIPSE
CONSTELLATION MILKY WAY   SPIRAL GALAXY
DWARF GALAXY   MOON   STAR
ELLIPTICAL GALAXY NEBULA   SUPERNOVA
FIREBALL   NOVA   WHITE DWARF

1. RSEDIATO _____
2. EHITW WADFR _____
3. SRAOL EPIECSL _____
4. VNAO _____
5. LIMYK WYA _____
6. ETOEMR _____
7. NTSAOOETNLLCI _____
8. ALRSIP GLAXYA _____
9. DRE ARWDF _____
10. IFERALBL _____
11. OMTCE _____
12. ALCIGTAC IKSD _____
13. PLEANT _____
14. NEULAB _____
15. AKBLC LHOE _____
16. DFRWA GYAXLA _____
17. NOOM _____
18. SART _____
19. UNPVAOSRE _____
20. ORMVIAWSCE _____
21. LALIELCIPT LYAGXA _____

"The Bible tells us the heavens declare God's glory....We certainly see that when we look into space. We see the beauty [and] we see the power [and] we see the majesty of God's hand revealed in what He's created."

— Jason Lisle, Ph.D., Astrophysics

"When you look at the Big Bang model, it's part of this overall evolutionary story where you have death and suffering going on for hundreds of millions of years...before man even appeared....How do you reconcile that with God's love for His creation?"

— Jake Hebert, Ph.D., Physics

Fun Fact:
The laws of physics describe the way that atoms and molecules are held together. If these laws were changed even slightly, life would be impossible.

Think Tank

1. Why is it important to understand that the past is something that cannot be observed by science?

   _____

   _____

   _____

2. Why do you think we have certain laws of physics that cannot be altered? What would science be like without them? _____

   _____

   _____

3. Summarize the Big Bang theory. _____

   _____

   _____

4. Why were secular scientists so excited in the 1960s when they detected microwave radiation coming from all directions in space? Explain the problems new research is finding with viewing this Cosmic Microwave Background radiation (CMB) as "proof" of the Big Bang. _____

   _____

   _____

   _____

5. What are some simple examples of how the laws of physics describe the order and precision that exist in our world—the opposite of the chaos that you would expect from an explosion? _____

   _____

   _____

6. How does the Second Law of Thermodynamics (the Law of Increasing Entropy) pose a powerful argument against the Big Bang? _____

   _____

   _____

   _____

Extraordinary Evidence

No humans witnessed the origin of life, and no physical geological evidence of its origin exists. But we can still derive facts that establish beyond doubt that an evolutionary origin of life on this planet would have been impossible.

Unimaginable Power

Beyond the power that lights the universe with stars is our Creator, who carefully balances the laws of nature. A star is a continuous explosion of awesome power. The power to create a universe with a billion galaxies, each with millions to trillions of stars, is beyond imagination. Creating mass and energy can only be done by a Creator who is outside nature.

The creation of the laws of nature themselves demonstrates an even greater power. These laws are balanced so that our sun provides energy to us day by day.

Exquisite Order

Light from stars and the sun begins with hydrogen—the most plentiful element in the universe. The sun is a large ball of very hot hydrogen more than 100 times larger than Earth. The sun's energy comes from hydrogen explosions. These are nuclear—much more powerful than chemical explosions. Gravity draws all the sun's hydrogen together, creating intense pressure. In the core of the sun, the huge forces cause nuclear fusion reactions. Hydrogen atoms fuse together into helium and release huge amounts of energy. These explosions do not cause the sun to suddenly blow up and then go cold. The balanced laws of physics hold our sun together. Gravity pulls the atoms back as each explosion pushes them away. This balance keeps the billions of stars in billions of galaxies burning.

Absolute Precision

If the laws of nature were just slightly different, the delicate balance required for hydrogen, oxygen, and carbon to react would not exist. Without this balance, thousands of vital molecular interactions would not happen. There are only a few elements with the properties that can sustain life. Changes to these elements would make life impossible.

Energy Can't Be Created or Destroyed

The Law of the Conservation of Energy (the First Law of Thermodynamics) says energy can't be created or destroyed; it can only be changed from one form to another. So, energy is not currently being created, and the universe could not have created itself using natural processes because nature did not exist before the universe. Something beyond nature must have created all the energy and matter we see today. Present measures of energy are so enormous that they indicate a power source that can only be described as "infinite."

> **Fun Fact:**
> The universe, as we know it, has over a hundred billion galaxies, each with millions to perhaps trillions of stars. There are also many different types of galaxies!

Adapted from Morris III, H. M. 2009. *Exploring the Evidence for Creation.* Dallas, TX: Institute for Creation Research.

For more extraordinary evidence, check out Guide to Creation Basics *and* Creation Basics & Beyond *at the ICR.org store!*

Back to the Bible

"Lift up your eyes on high, and see who has created these things, who brings out their host by number; He calls them all by name, by the greatness of His might and the strength of His power; not one is missing."

— Isaiah 40:26

Read

Genesis 1 • Genesis 8:22 • Psalm 74:16 • Isaiah 40:26 • James 1:17

Respond

1. List everything you observe in these verses that shows us how the universe holds together and how it operates. _____ _____

2. On which creation day did God create space, time, matter, and energy? _____

3. What does the First Law of Thermodynamics tell us about the original energy that God put into the universe?_____

4. How do Genesis 8:22 and Isaiah 40:26 support the Law of Conservation of Mass and Energy (the First Law of Thermodynamics)? _____ _____

5. What does the Law of Entropy show us about whether the universe could be eternally old? _____ _____

6. If the universe is not eternal, it had to have a beginning. As we know from simple logic, every beginning requires what? What "law" applies here?_____ _____

7. What does it mean that God has "no variation or shadow of turning" (James 1:17)? How can this statement apply to our universe…and our everyday lives?_____ _____ _____

Takeaways

- Our universe has order—not chaos—because it was designed with order and purpose by the Creator God who does not change, who is always consistent.
- The laws of physics and mathematics reflect the order and purpose God instilled in His creation.
- Even though we were not there at the beginning to observe the creation of the universe, scientific evidence indicates that Earth is young and that every detail of our universe was planned—it was not an accident.

Awesome Activities for All Ages

1. **Homemade play dough**

    As a family: Make homemade play dough, and have students create whatever inspires them. Talk about how the play dough did not come from "nothing" and how they used a plan, order, and design to end up with their "creation."

2. **Picnic time**

    As a group: Take a picnic to a local park or lake. Have each student take their sketchbook, pick one spot to stay in, and list and illustrate all of the things they can see that show order and design from where they're sitting.

3. **Laws of Physics day**

    Older Students: Create a point and award system for every time students name which law they are operating under as they go throughout the day.

4. **Order from chaos?**

    Order never comes from chaos but always (either directly or indirectly) from intent. Build a car using interconnected plastic blocks or a construction set, then test it to make sure it rolls. Disassemble it and place its parts into a plastic bag or box. Shake it.

    a. If we shook the bag for a million years, could those parts reassemble themselves into a working car? What would eventually happen to the bag or box or parts before any of them ever self-assembled?

    b. List organized features of the cosmos. (For example, stars, planets, orbits, solar systems, galaxies, galactic clusters, magnetic fields, etc.) Just like the car, what kind of assembly would these features require?

5. **Order matters**

    Illustrate the importance of an orderly cosmos by trying to play a game without rules. Use a deck of cards to play a game, but make sure the game has only one rule: It cannot use rules. Is this setup fun? Next, play a card game that has rules.

    a. What do we call the "rules" by which the universe operates? (natural laws/laws of physics)

    b. How were game rules invented—by accident or on purpose? What does this indicate about the rules that describe the natural forces governing our universe?

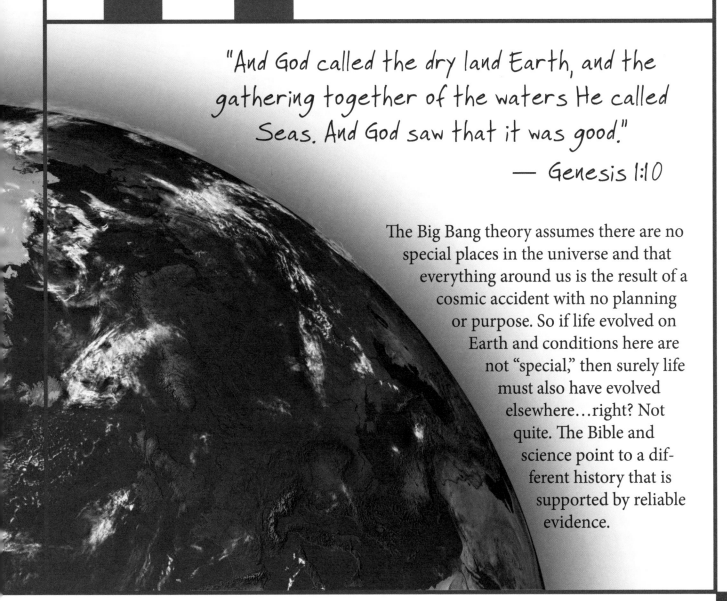

Episode 11 Uniqueness of Earth

The universe holds many galaxies with countless suns, stars, and probably planets as well, but evidence shows that Earth is unique among them all.

"And God called the dry land Earth, and the gathering together of the waters He called Seas. And God saw that it was good."

— Genesis 1:10

The Big Bang theory assumes there are no special places in the universe and that everything around us is the result of a cosmic accident with no planning or purpose. So if life evolved on Earth and conditions here are not "special," then surely life must also have evolved elsewhere…right? Not quite. The Bible and science point to a different history that is supported by reliable evidence.

Brainy Buzzwords

Life on Other Planets?

Using the word bank below, fill in the blanks. Some words may be used more than once!

400	giants	Neptune	spiral
carbon	life	Pluto	sun
cold	lifeless	rock	terrestrial
dwarf	light	Saturn	thin
Earth	long	seven	Venus
evidence	Mars	size	water
galaxy	Mercury	smaller	
gas	Milky	solar	

1. In our solar system, Earth joins _____ other planets in orbit around a giant _____. Our _____ system is part of a _____ galaxy called the _____ Way, and it's been estimated that there are between 100 and _____ billion stars in this galaxy alone. We're located on one arm of the spiral and around 27,000 _____ years from the center of the _____.

2. The planets closest to the sun are called _____ planets because they're composed mostly of _____ and metals. Nearest the sun is Mercury, then _____ and of course Earth—the third planet out—and then _____.

3. The four outer planets are the gas _____ made primarily of gas and frozen vapor. These are Jupiter, _____, Uranus, and _____. Poor _____, which lost its planet status in 2006, is now classified as a _____ planet.

4. However, out of all of these, _____ is the only one of the bodies in our solar system capable of sustaining _____.

5. _____ is closest to the sun and has no atmosphere. That, plus the extremely high temperatures on its _____-facing side, makes it unwelcoming to _____.

6. Venus is about the same _____ as Earth, but it has a dense, hot atmosphere that's mostly _____ dioxide. You won't find _____ there.

7. Mars has always seemed a likely candidate for life. A day there is about as _____ as one here. But it's _____ than Earth, and the atmosphere is too _____ to sustain life. The air on Mars has only about 1/1,000 as much _____ as our air.

8. Jupiter is a big ball of _____, and we wouldn't want to live there. We've found no _____ of life on any of its moons.

9. Saturn is also a _____ sphere of gas, and its moons appear to be barren, _____ places.

10. Uranus and Neptune are gas _____ too, and _____ is just ice. None of these are going to have _____.

Brainy Buzzwords

Earth: No Place Like Home

Unscramble the letters below to reveal these "spacey" terms!

ASTRONOMY   GOLDILOCKS ZONE   ORBIT   TELESCOPE
DWARF PLANET   JUPITER   PLANET   TILT
EARTH   MARS   PLUTO   URANUS
EXPLOSION   MERCURY   SATURN   VENUS
FLARE   MILKY WAY   SOLAR SYSTEM
GALAXY   MOON   SPACECRAFT
GAS GIANT   NEPTUNE   SPHERICAL

1. ETRJIPU _____

2. TPUOL _____

3. NRSATU _____

4. SAG TNIAG _____

5. IHRCEPSLA _____

6. LFREA _____

7. HRATE _____

8. OIRBT _____

9. CATEAFCSRP _____

10. MASR _____

11. TSEECLEOP _____

12. UNVES _____

13. FWARD NALPET _____

14. AYMONTSOR _____

15. ILTT _____

16. XYLAAG _____

17. SARUNU _____

18. EPISOXLNO _____

19. NPTUEEN _____

20. ILKYM YAW _____

21. NAETLP _____

22. OMON _____

23. ROSLA METSYS _____

24. MYCEURR _____

25. KLOCSOLDIG EONZ _____

89

"When we look into the universe, we see all kinds of planets out there, but none of them that are as unique as Earth."

— Jason Lisle, Ph.D., Astrophysics

"The question here is not whether or not the laws of physics and chemistry permit life to exist. Obviously, they do or none of us would be here….The real issue is, do the laws of physics and chemistry in our universe…permit life to come from non-life?…All of our scientific observations are indicating that the answer is no."

— Jake Hebert, Ph.D., Physics

Fun Fact:
It's been estimated that there are between 100 and 400 billion stars in the Milky Way alone!

Think Tank

1. How are the planets in our solar system categorized, and what are their characteristics? _____
   _____
   _____

2. What is the "Goldilocks zone"? _____
   _____

3. What do secular scientists really hope to find on another planet? Even if they found it, why would that not be enough to prove that life could exist there? _____
   _____
   _____

4. What is the significance of Kepler-22b? _____
   _____
   _____

5. List three examples of why the seven other planets are unsuitable for life. _____
   _____
   _____

6. What makes Earth unique and perfect for sustaining life? List everything you can think of—use the scientific facts you know. _____
   _____

7. Why is it "wishful thinking" for some scientists to say there is life on other planets? _____
   _____
   _____

8. Astronomer and evolutionist Carl Sagan said, "We find that we live on an insignificant planet of a humdrum star lost in a galaxy tucked away in some forgotten corner of a universe in which there are far more galaxies than people" (Sagan, C. 1980. *Cosmos*. New York: Random House, 159). How would this outlook affect someone's view of life? _____
   _____

9. What are some of the strongest pieces of evidence you would choose to explain how unique Earth really is?_____
   _____

Extraordinary Evidence

How can we know that Earth was perfectly created for life? What makes it unique? Does science confirm what the Bible says about God's unique creation?

Living Organisms

Most significantly, Earth is the only planet known to contain living organisms. And they can be found everywhere. In virtually every environment on this planet, we discover creatures that flourish. This greatly contrasts with the lifeless, barren surfaces of the other planets in our solar system. Many of Earth's other unique qualities seem to be specifically designed to support such life.

Water

Over 70 percent of Earth is covered with liquid water. No other known planet has such an abundance of water. Since water is an essential requirement for all known life, the presence of water on Earth seems to be a key design feature. Earth orbits at the ideal distance from the sun for temperatures to allow for liquid water and has an atmospheric pressure just right for liquid water.

Atmosphere

Earth's atmosphere has a protective layer of ozone that partially blocks ultraviolet radiation. This too appears to be a design feature since such radiation can be very damaging to living tissue. Unlike Venus, Earth has a strong magnetic field. This field deflects harmful cosmic radiation, protecting inhabitants on Earth's surface.

Tilt

Earth is tilted on its axis 23.4 degrees relative to its orbit around the sun, causing our planet to experience seasons. This tilt appears to be well designed for life. If Earth were tilted less, the polar regions would receive less energy, reducing the livable area of the planet. If the earth were tilted more, the seasons would become more extreme, potentially reducing plant-growing seasons and making the environment less hospitable. However, the seasons are *not* caused by Earth's slightly elliptical orbit. On the contrary, Earth is actually slightly closer to the sun in the northern hemisphere winter.[1]

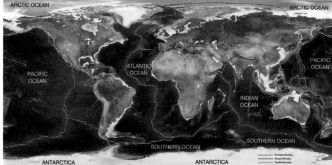

Plate Tectonics

Earth is the only planet known to have plate tectonics. (Tectonics is the geology field that studies processes that deform Earth's crust.) While other planets have tectonic activity as evidenced by volcanoes, their crusts are not divided into plates. Many creation scientists believe that Earth's continents were connected before the global Flood and moved apart during the Flood year. Geophysicist John Baumgardner's model of runaway subduction explains the global Flood of Noah's day in terms of catastrophic plate tectonics that apparently took place during the Flood year.[2] It appears that God constructed Earth with the built-in capacity to produce and experience a global flood. None of the other planets have substantial liquid water at present, and even if they did, they would have no mechanism for runaway subduction.

Adapted from Lisle, J. 2013. The Solar System: Earth and Moon. *Acts & Facts.* 42 (10): 10. *Endnotes included in Answer Key.*

For more extraordinary evidence, check out The Solar System: God's Heavenly Handiwork *at the ICR.org store!*

> **Fun Fact:**
> Did you know Earth is 8,000 miles in diameter and weighs around 6.6 sextillion tons?

Back to the Bible

"For thus says the LORD, who created the heavens, who is God, who formed the earth and made it, who has established it, who did not create it in vain, who formed it to be inhabited."

— Isaiah 45:18

Read

Genesis 1:9-10 • Genesis 1:16 • Genesis 1:20-21 • Job 26:7 • Isaiah 40:22 • Isaiah 45:18

Respond

1. According to the Bible, why did God create the earth? So, who do you think He really created it for?

   _____

   _____

2. What details about Earth's physical shape and position can we learn from these verses? How is the Bible's description of Earth supported by science? _____

   _____

3. How do we know that there were specific, separate purposes for the creation of the sun and moon?

   _____

   _____

4. How long did God spend creating Earth? What does this say about its value? _____

   _____

5. What do these verses tell us about the order and planning that went into creation? _____

   _____

6. What was God's attitude toward His final product? _____

7. What security can we take in knowing *why* God created and *how* He created? How should this knowledge affect our view of ourselves, others, and life in general? _____

   _____

Takeaways

- The Bible is clear that God created the earth with great care and for a specific purpose—to sustain life—and He is in complete control.
- The order, planning, and detail that God put into making our planet livable gives us worth and proclaims His glory.
- Scripture tells us that some people will choose not to see the hand of God in the world all around us (Romans 1; 2 Peter 3:5-7). What can our role be in changing that?

Awesome Activities for All Ages

1. Kepler-22b

Older students: Further research Kepler-22b. Reference these articles at ICR.org: "Another Goldilocks Planet Stirs ET Hopes" and "SETI Radio Telescope Goes Back Online." Identify key barriers to this planet's ability to sustain life.

2. Perfect for life

As a group: Create and illustrate a chart of physical evidence that Earth was optimized for life.

3. Planetarium trip

As a family: Take a field trip to the planetarium. Watch for a great visual of how stars, planets, and galaxies all interconnect. Try to find an exhibit where you can experience looking through a telescope. Be sure to have students identify and talk through any information in the planetarium presentation that might contradict what the Bible and science tell us about Earth's origins. Use the creation planetarium DVD available at the ICR.org store as a comparison to the secular planetarium show.

4. Build your own terrarium

Find and follow instructions on how to build a two-liter terrarium. Experiment by building terrariums that are missing critical features, like a plant that converts CO_2 to oxygen or a transparent border that lets light in. After a few weeks, compare the terrariums and discuss how they mimic Earth's life-friendly features in the context of Isaiah 45:18.

5. Earth from space

Creation advocate and NASA astronaut Colonel Jeff Williams has taken thousands of photographs of Earth from the International Space Station, and many of his images are archived online in "The Gateway to Astronaut Photography of Earth" (eol.jsc.nasa.gov). Browse some images, especially in the "Collections" category titled "Earth from Space." Compare the photos of Earth to Job 26:7 and Isaiah 40:22. Does the Bible accurately describe what we can observe through science?

1 ¹In the beginning God created the
heaven and the earth.
2 And the earth was without form,
and void; and darkness was upon the
face of the deep. And the Spirit of
God moved upon the face of the waters.
3 And God said, Let there be light:
and there was light.
4 And God saw the light, that it
was good: and God divided the light
from the darkness.
And God called the light Day,
and the darkness he called Night.
And the evening and the morning
were the first day.
And God said, Let there be a
firmament in the midst of the waters,
and let it divide the waters from the
waters.

lights in the firmament of the
to divide the day from the nig
let them be for signs, and for s
and for days, and years:
15 And let them be for lights in
firmament of the heaven to giv
upon the earth: and it was so.
16 And God made two great
the greater light to rule the d
the lesser light to rule the
made the stars also.
17 And God set them in the firmament of the heaven to give
the earth.

GENESIS

12

Science and Scripture

Within every human is a deep need to answer questions about their origins. Where do we come from? How did life begin? Is there a God? Why are we here? Contrary to what many people believe, the Bible and science work together to help answer these questions. You don't have to choose one over the other.

"For since the creation of the world His invisible attributes are clearly seen, being understood by the things that are made, even His eternal power and Godhead, so that they are without excuse."

— Romans 1:20

For centuries, Christians found answers in the Bible, without question. There was little or no perceived conflict between science and Scripture. Today, things aren't so simple. Christians still find answers in the Bible, the Word of God. But many Christians question if the Bible is completely true. It is. And we can rely on the Bible as an accurate record of creation. We can believe it all, not just some of it.

Brainy Buzzwords

Beginnings Matter

Using the word bank below, fill in the blanks. Some words may be used more than once!

accident	design	gift	meaning	winged
beginning	designed	good	moon	world
Bible	Designer	herbs	night	years
big	die	land	purpose	
chemical	earth	life	reason	
creatures	eternal	Lord	soup	
death	Genesis	man	system	

1. We began this journey with a basic question—was the world _____ by God, or did it just happen? Secular science attributes all of creation to a lucky break—a random chance, a cosmic _____ that resulted in _____ forming on Earth. It's a rather bleak perspective on _____ and death. We're born; we _____. Our brief time alive on this planet comes and goes without _____.

2. But when Christians look at the complexity and beauty of the _____, we see a world that is designed with order, _____, purpose, and _____.

3. Remember the hummingbird and the mimic octopus that can disguise itself to look like many other _____? Those aren't random. Even the simplest of cells is complex and shows _____. And to be designed, they need a _____.

4. The _____ describes the real account of how _____ began in Genesis:
   In the _____, God created the heavens and the _____. He made the light and divided it from the darkness and created a firmament to divide the waters. He established the _____ and seas and grass, _____, and trees. He created lights in the heavens to divide day from _____ and to be for signs and seasons, days and _____. He put in place the sun, _____, and stars and created the creatures of the sea, _____ birds, and land animals, each according to its kind. And last, He created _____ in His own image and likeness. And then God saw everything He had made and indeed it was very _____.

5. Chapter one of _____ explains all of creation—the planet, the solar _____, our atmosphere, and us—not creation of the universe by a _____ bang or the creation of life by a random _____ accident in a primordial _____.

6. What we observe today supports what the Bible says about our origins. Which worldview will you believe? Which one is true? The one in which _____ is the end and your life is without _____? Or, the one that believes in God the Creator, says _____ has a higher purpose, and in which "the _____ of God is _____ life in Christ Jesus our _____" (Romans 6:23).

Brainy Buzzwords

The Big Picture

See how quickly you can find all of these words hidden in the puzzle below. Words may be spelled vertically, horizontally, diagonally, or backward.

ACCIDENT   COVENANT   NATURALISTIC   SCOFFERS
ANCESTOR   DESIGN   OMNIPOTENT   SECULAR
ARCHAEOLOGY   DIVERSITY   OMNISCIENT   SOVEREIGN
ATTRIBUTES   EYEWITNESS   PURPOSE   SUPERNATURAL
BELIEVE   IMAGE   RANDOM   THEOLOGIAN
COSMIC   INVISIBLE   SCIENTIST   WORLDVIEW

```
S C O F F E R S I S O T M R N V L
S A O V N R A L U C E S N I R I L
E L N V S W O R L D V I E W M S Y
S R A C E T M N I Y I T S A T N S
A U C O E N N E E G P N G I S E D
S Y P C F S A E A O B E L I E V E
V S V E U A T N T L C I M S O C E
L N S S R W U O T O A C S S T R E
D G I E C N R G R E P S E R H E T
T I N R N T A F I A U I A N E B S
N E V E I T L T B H E N N O O A E
S R I E E O I T U C M M D M L S O
M E S N R C S W T R E O T I O E B
O V I R L S T U E A A E D P G I I
G O B O A N I O S Y G L R N I E V
E S L O Y E C T O A E U N I A R G
T N E D I C C A Y D P E S I N R L
```

"Some people have said, 'Why does it really matter why we believe in six days or millions of years?' If the Bible is wrong about the timescale of creation, then how we can we trust it on other matters?...So, it really does matter."

— Jason Lisle, Ph.D., Astrophysics

"What we observe today in the world is absolutely consistent with God's Word—that He created organisms fully functioning."

— Georgia Purdom, Ph.D., Molecular Genetics

"It's not just the external physical capacities that you see that make us different. Clearly, there is a major difference between humans and chimpanzees....Humans put men on the moon. Humans build hospitals. Humans use surgical instruments and operate on each other. Humans play baseball and go to ballets and write poetry."

—Randy Guliuzza, P.E., M.D.

Think Tank

1. You've seen the evidence from both sides—creation and evolution. Which one presents the stronger argument? Which side presents the more popular argument? Why? _____

   _____

   _____

2. What are some basic differences between evolution and creation when it comes to views on God, life, and death? _____

   _____

3. What makes us different from chimpanzees and indicates we *do not* have a common ancestor, based both on observations and on the Bible? _____

   _____

4. Why is Noah's Flood so significant for what we believe about origins? _____

   _____

5. Why is it important whether dinosaurs lived and died before humans or whether they lived with humans? _____

   _____

6. What in Scripture indicates that God created in six days, which supports the theory that Earth is only thousands of years old? _____

   _____

7. Why does it matter if the earth is billions of years old or only a few thousand, like the Bible says?

   _____

   _____

8. Economic and social theorist Jeremy Rifkin said, "It is our creation now. We make the rules. We establish the parameters of reality. We create the world, and because we do, we no longer feel beholden to outside forces. We no longer have to justify our behavior, for we are now the architects of the universe. We are responsible to nothing outside ourselves, for we are the kingdom, the power, and the glory for ever and ever" (Rifkin, J. 1983. *Algeny*. New York: Viking Press, 298). How would believing this shape the way someone looks at life? _____

   _____

   _____

Extraordinary Evidence

What we believe about where we came from, how life began, if there is a God, and why we are here shapes our entire outlook on life and where we will spend eternity. That's why these questions have been so important to man since the beginning of time and why we should be so careful and thoughtful about how we choose to answer them.

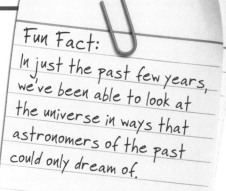

Fun Fact:
In just the past few years, we've been able to look at the universe in ways that astronomers of the past could only dream of.

Contrasting Worldviews

The obvious "good and evil" conflict in every culture throughout all recorded time is expressed and explained clearly in the Bible. Buried deep inside every human are timeless questions that surface frequently and suddenly throughout our lifetime. Everybody capable of rational thought thinks these things—no exceptions:

- Who am I? (identity)
- Why am I here? (purpose)
- What is going to happen to me? (future, life after death)
- Where did I come from, and how and when did all this start? (origins)

No human being operates without a bias, a tendency to believe one idea over another. The naturalist believes that there is no such thing as a supernatural force and that man has reached the stage in history where he is able to direct the evolutionary development of the universe. The creationist believes that a Creator God exists and that all of His creatures must seek to understand His will.

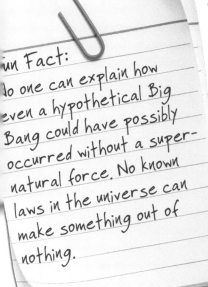

Fun Fact:
No one can explain how even a hypothetical Big Bang could have possibly occurred without a supernatural force. No known laws in the universe can make something out of nothing.

These "believers" share some common data, but they will interpret it through their own belief system—their worldview or faith. When we ask the questions that plague our minds (Why is the world so full of evil? Why can't we all get along? Is it always going to be this way?), the answers come from our worldview. What we believe frames our reactions, our priorities, and our expectations. The Bible describes the many parts of worldviews in their simplest and most fundamental form: truth or lie.

The ultimate contrast is between the revelation of the Creator God who cannot lie (Hebrews 6:18) and the great adversary, Satan, who is the "father" of the lie (John 8:44). The Bible provides a comprehensive and logically consistent body of answers and explanations to all of the critical worldview issues: who (including Who), what, where, when, how, and why. In fact, Scripture even explains why we have such different viewpoints. The Bible also predicts cause-and-effect connections between the worldview we have, the actions we take in life, and the impact of those actions, both here and in the hereafter.

In his article "The Abolition of Truth and Morality," well-known philosopher Dr. Francis Schaeffer observed the following about the naturalistic and Christian worldviews: "These two world views stand as totals in complete antithesis to each other in content and also in their natural results" (churchleadership.org). One view offers a life with meaning, salvation in Jesus Christ, and hope based on the Bible that is confirmed by scientific evidence. The other relies on the wisdom of man and emphasizes that life has no purpose. Which future do you want for yourself? Which will you believe?

Adapted from Morris III, H. M. 2009. *Exploring the Evidence for Creation.* Dallas, TX: Institute for Creation Research.

For more extraordinary evidence, check out Discerning Truth *or* The Ultimate Proof of Creation *at the ICR.org store!*

Back to the Bible

> "The heaven, even the heavens, are the
> LORD's; but the earth He has given to the
> children of men."
>
> — Psalm 115:16

Read

Genesis 1:16 • Psalm 19:1 • Psalm 115:16 • John 3:12 • Acts 17:26 • Romans 1:20 • 1 Corinthians 15:41
2 Peter 3:4-5

Respond

1. How does the historical and scientific evidence confirm what the Bible says in Acts 17:26?
   _____

2. One of the most controversial topics in the debate between evolution and creation is how the universe began. No one can explain how even a hypothetical Big Bang could have possibly occurred without a supernatural force. What is the explanation that Genesis 1:16, Psalm 19:1, and 1 Corinthians 15:41 offer?
   _____

3. What did Jesus mean by his statement in John 3:12, and how does that apply to the origins debate?
   _____

4. What is a worldview? Define your personal worldview. _____

5. What does Romans 1:20 say about what we can know about God, even if someone does not have a relationship with Him? _____

6. Based on 2 Peter 3:4-5, what do people "willfully forget"? What specific worldview is hinted at in these verses? _____

7. What are some of the main differences between a naturalist worldview and a creationist worldview? What are some potential consequences of choosing the naturalistic viewpoint? _____
   _____

8. Nothing we can see in our Earth contradicts Psalm 115:16. If you believe this, how should it change your life? _____

Takeaways

- The differences between a creationist worldview and a naturalist worldview are huge. One offers hope based on the truth of the Bible, salvation in Jesus Christ, and a Bible that is confirmed by scientific evidence. The other relies on the wisdom of man and emphasizes that life has no purpose.
- As Christians, we have an important role in sharing the truth about creation.
- Think about your friends, the activities you're involved in, and your life goals. How can you take those opportunities and use them to talk about how science and the Bible work together to give us truth, hope, and purpose?

Awesome Activities for All Ages

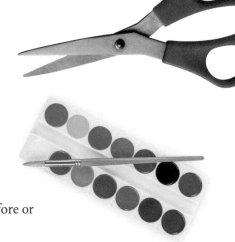

1. Why creation?

Younger students: Write out and illustrate Psalm 115:16.

Older students: Pick *one* of the key points of tension between evolution and creation—the Big Bang, uniformitarianism/catastrophism, the common ancestor, etc.—and outline the different concepts in a short essay. At the end of the essay, include a strategy for how you would share this truth of science and Scripture with a friend who may never have heard this information before or who does not share your worldview.

2. Share the evidence

As a family: Host a "Creation Night" and invite neighbors, family, and friends over to enjoy a creative presentation highlighting one or two key topics that have been covered in this series. Consider showing your favorite *Unlocking the Mysteries of Genesis* episode as part of the presentation. Let each student help in the planning of the program and share something they have learned. Use this as a teaching tool for how a fun time of fellowship can be used to share truth and perhaps even the gospel itself!

3. A solid foundation

As a group: Play the game Jenga®. As the game is going on and after the tower falls, answer these questions: If your Jenga® tower represents your worldview, what happens when things begin to chip away at what you think you believe? What can you do to make sure your worldview has a solid foundation?

4. What most scientists say

Older students: Select an excerpt from a secular textbook or article that discusses origins—of animals, man, Earth, or the cosmos. Do scientists use the same techniques to answer questions about how things *work* as they do when answering questions about how things *began*? What level of confidence should we place in "scientific" theories compared to eyewitness origins accounts? To which of those categories does Genesis belong? (See the article: "The Biblical Hebrew Creation Account: New Numbers Tell the Story" at ICR.org)

5. The gospel and Genesis

As a family: Discuss and describe how each of these four core elements of the gospel finds its origins in Genesis:

a. We have done wrong and deserve punishment.

b. We are accountable to God for wrongdoing.

c. Being born as one of us, Jesus did no wrong yet suffered our just punishment for us.

d. By trusting Christ, we are saved from our just penalty and receive everlasting life.

6. Paul was a creationist

As a family: Read Acts 14 and Acts 17. Consider how the apostle Paul used creation to introduce the Creator and His good news. As a missionary, why did he choose to emphasize creation? How can we learn from Paul and consider the way we do or don't talk about creation with people around us?

If God did create everything as described in the book of Genesis, when did He do it? On a timescale, how do we get from the beginning of creation to now?

KEY
AC — After Creation

CREATION

Birth of
Seth
(Gen. 5:3)

Birth of
Noah
(Gen. 7:11)

Noah Builds
Ark
(Gen 6:3)

Flood
(Gen. 8:13)

Tower of
Babel
(Gen. 10:25; 11:9)

Ice Age
~1900-2200 A

0 AC*   ~130 AC   ~1056 AC   ~1536 AC   ~1656 AC   ~1900 AC

*Dates are approximations. Not to scale.

Bonus
Episode

"Then God spoke to Noah, saying, 'Go out of the ark, you and your wife, and your sons and your sons' wives with you. Bring out with you every living thing of all flesh that is with you: birds and cattle and every creeping thing that creeps on the earth, so that they may abound on the earth, and be fruitful and multiply on the earth."
— Genesis 8:15-17

Fun Fact:
Before the Flood, humans had much longer lifespans than today.

Birth of Abraham
(Gen. 11:10-27)

Abraham Travels into Egypt
(Gen. 12:4-10)

Birth of Christ
(Matt. 21; Luke 1:5; 2:1)

~2000 AC ~2100 AC

~4000 AC

Brainy Buzzwords

Now and Then

Using the word bank and the timeline on the previous page, fill in the blanks about some of these key dates in our history from creation through today.

300	earth	Lord
371	Egypt	pyramids
1,056	father	Tower of Babel
1,536	Flood	Ur
2100	God	zero
4,000	Ice Age	
Ark	language	

> "There are many linguistic and archaeological discoveries that confirm the reliability of the biblical text. One of the spectacular examples is of the discovery of the Dead Sea Scrolls….One of the outcomes of that finding was to demonstrate a very high degree of accuracy of the copies of the full text of the Old Testament that we have today."
>
> — Leslie P. Bruce, Ph.D., Linguistics

1. In the beginning—year _____—God created Adam and Eve and all the living things of the _____.

2. Noah was born around _____ years after creation.

3. Around _____ years after creation, God instructed Noah to build the _____.

4. The _____ came and lasted _____ days, about 1,656 years after creation, or roughly around 2500 B.C.

5. The major climate-related effect of the Flood—what we know now to be the _____ _____— started around 200 years after the Flood and lasted about _____ years. *

6. During this time, mankind again became wicked, exalting man over _____ and building the _____ _____ _____ to reach to heaven. Because of their defiance, God confused their _____ and dispersed them.

7. In _____ B.C., not quite 2,000 years after creation, Abraham, the "_____ of many nations," was born in the city of _____ of the Chaldees.

8. When Abraham traveled into _____, around 2000 B.C., the _____ were already standing.

9. About _____ years after creation, in the Year of Our _____, Jesus Christ our Savior was born.

And the rest is history!

"Every word of God is pure; He is a shield to those who put their trust in Him."

— Proverbs 30:5

* Endnotes included in Answer Key.

Fun Fact:
By the end of the Ice Age, the world's population had grown to one million people...or more!

Takeaways

- When we research and see how the timeline of the Bible lines up with actual historical events and evidence uncovered by archaeologists, it reinforces our confidence in God's Word and His promises. And just like the historical evidence, we have seen that the scientific evidence we have today also supports God's Word as true. What should our response be?

> "I will bless the Lord at all times; His praise shall continually be in my mouth. My soul shall make its boast in the Lord; the humble shall hear of it and be glad. Oh, magnify the Lord with me, and let us exalt His name together." — Psalm 34:1-3

> Tell the world!

Resources

Reading Corner

Visit ICR.org and explore our extensive publication database. Search by title to access the articles below, as well as other news and research relating to each episode's topic. You can also acquire the books listed and other resources by visiting our online store.

Websites

ICR.org — Science news, articles, resources, and calendar of nationwide speaking events

UnlockingTheMysteriesOfGenesis.org — Background, episode clips, and links to purchase

YourOriginsMatter.com — Student-geared origins articles, blogs, videos, and social media

TeachAllThings.org — Sermon outlines and searchable articles

Episode 1

Books

Guide to Creation Basics

The Design and Complexity of the Cell

Creation Basics & Beyond

Exploring the Evidence for Creation

Six Days of Creation

Is the Big Bang Biblical?

5 Reasons to Believe in Recent Creation

Biblical Creationism

The Ultimate Proof of Creation

Your Origins Matter

The Genesis Record

Articles at ICR.org

Evolution of Life Research Close to Creation

What Will the Next Biological Breakthrough Be?

Baylor Surgeon "Dissects" Darwinism

New Life Origins Theory Has Old Problems

Evaluating Real vs. Apparent Design

Fit & Function: Design in Nature

"Natural" Selection Versus "Supernatural" Design

DVD

The Secret Code of Creation

Episode 2

Books

Guide to Creation Basics

Guide to Animals

The Design and Complexity of the Cell

Clearly Seen: Constructing Solid Arguments for Design

The Ocean Book

Exploring the Evidence for Creation

Creation Basics & Beyond

The Book of Beginnings, Volume 1: Creation, Fall, and the First Age

Biology and the Bible

Six Days of Creation

The Genesis Record

Articles at ICR.org

Could Space Dust Help Spark Life?

It's (Virtually) Alive!

First Cell's Survival Odds Not in Evolution's Favor

Could a Virus Jump-Start the First Cell?

Historic "Primordial Soup" Study Yields New Data, But Not New Answers

Biology and the Bible

What Is the Origin of Life?

Episode 3

Books

Made in His Image

The Design and Complexity of the Cell

Guide to Creation Basics

Biology and the Bible

Creation Basics & Beyond

The Book of Beginnings, Volume 1: Creation, Fall, and the First Age

Six Days of Creation

Exploring the Evidence for Creation
Your Origins Matter
The Genesis Record

Articles at ICR.org

Human and Chimp DNA—Nearly Identical?
Using ENCODE Data for Human-Chimp DNA Comparisons
Stark Differences Between Human and Chimp Brains
Similar Features Show Design, Not Universal Common Descent
Recent Human Variation Is Not Evolution
Study Shows Humans Are Uniquely Designed for Music
Why High-Speed Throwing Is Uniquely Human
Scientists Get Glimpse into Infant Language Learning

DVD

Human Design: The Making of a Baby (Note: parents may want to preview)

Episode 4

Books

The Global Flood
The Fossil Record
Guide to Creation Basics
The Geology Book
Earth's Catastrophic Past
The Genesis Flood
Bones of Contention
The Book of Beginnings, Volume 2: Noah, the Flood, and the New World
Exploring the Evidence for Creation
Creation Basics & Beyond

Articles at ICR.org

The Real Nature of the Fossil Record
The Vanishing Case for Evolution
Live Birth Fossil Exposes Evolutionary Enigma
Flower Fossils 100,000,000 Years Out of Place?
Did Some Dinosaurs Really Have Feathers?
Is the Cambrian Explosion Problem Solved?

Scan of Amber-Trapped Spider Shows Recent Origin

Extraordinary Mosasaur Fossil Reveals Original Soft Tissues

Episode 5

Books

The Global Flood

Guide to Creation Basics

Guide to Animals

Noah's Ark: A Feasibility Study

The Geology Book

The Genesis Flood

Earth's Catastrophic Past

The Genesis Record

Exploring the Evidence for Creation

Creation Basics & Beyond

The Book of Beginnings, Volume 2: Noah, the Flood, and the New World

Footprints in the Ash

Articles at ICR.org

The Vital Doctrine of a Global Flood

Genesis Flood Insights More Relevant Today than Ever

Slot Canyons, a Stunning Flood Formation

Why Does Nearly Every Culture Have a Tradition of a Global Flood?

Japan Tsunami Demonstrates Destructive Power of Water

Continents Didn't Drift, They Raced

30 Years Later, the Lessons from Mount St. Helens

Shark Jaw Opens Questions about Coal Formation

DVD

Mount St. Helens

Episode 6

Books

The Young Earth

The Fossil Record

Guide to Creation Basics

The Geology Book

5 Reasons to Believe in Recent Creation

The Global Flood

Earth's Catastrophic Past

Exploring the Evidence for Creation

Creation Basics & Beyond

The Book of Beginnings, Volume 1: Creation, Fall, and the First Age

The Book of Beginnings, Volume 2: Noah, the Flood, and the New World

Articles at ICR.org

Why Recent Creation Matters

How Does Old Earth Thinking Affect One's View of Scripture's Reliability?

New Genetic-Clock Research Challenges Millions of Years

Age of Grand Canyon Remains a Mystery

Counting Earth's Age in Lightning Strikes

Rethinking Carbon-14 Dating: What Does It Really Tell Us about the Age of the Earth?

Bloody Mosquito Fossil Supports Recent Creation

Understanding Evidence for the Biblical Timescale

DVD

Mount St. Helens

Episode 7

Books

Dinosaurs and the Bible

Guide to Animals

Guide to Creation Basics

Untold Secrets of Planet Earth: Dire Dragons

Dinosaurs by Design

Dragons: Legends & Lore of Dinosaurs

The Fossil Record

Creation Basics & Beyond

Exploring the Evidence for Creation

Articles at ICR.org

Did Dinosaurs Survive the Flood?

Eyewitnesses to Extinction: Testimonies to the Life and Death of Dinosaurs

The Dinosaur Next Door

Dinosaurs According to Their Creator

Amber Fossils Redefine "Age of Reptiles"

Jungle-Covered Ruins May Hold Surprising Hints

Triceratops Horn Soft Tissue Foils "Biofilm" Explanation

Did Scientists Find *T. Rex* DNA?

T. Rex Toddler Answers Noah's Ark Questions

DVDs

What You Haven't Been Told About Dinosaurs

Dragons or Dinosaurs?

Episode 8

Books

The Ice Age and the Flood

Guide to Creation Basics

The Global Flood

The Geology Book

Earth's Catastrophic Past

The Genesis Flood

Footprints in the Ash

Exploring the Evidence for Creation

Creation Basics & Beyond

The Book of Beginnings, Volume 2: Noah, the Flood, and the New World

Articles at ICR.org

Was There an Ice Age?

The Ice Age: Causes and Consequences

Speedy Glaciers Trample Multiple Ice-Age Theories

Ancient Lake Bed Merges with Biblical Clues

Over 100 Frozen Original Mammoth Proteins Found

What Caused the Extinction of Ice Age Animals?

Mummified Forest Highlights Post-Flood Ice Age

Ancient Wooden Door Has "Remarkable" Design

DVD

Mount St. Helens

Episode 9

Books

Guide to Creation Basics

The Fossil Record

The Global Flood

Exploring the Evidence for Creation

Creation Basics & Beyond

The Book of Beginnings, Volume 2: Noah, the Flood, and the New World

The Genesis Record

Bones of Contention

Earth's Catastrophic Past

The Genesis Flood

Articles at ICR.org

Evolution and Modern Racism

Where Did the Races Come From?

The Dispersal at Babel

DNA Proof That Neandertals Are Just Humans

Does "Y-Chromosome Adam" Refute Genesis?

Genetics Research Confirms Biblical Timeline

African Populations Fit Biblical History

Human Languages Fit a Young Earth Model

Episode 10

Books

Guide to Creation Basics

The Stargazer's Guide to the Night Sky

Is the Big Bang Biblical?

Taking Back Astronomy

Creation Basics & Beyond

Exploring the Evidence for Creation

The Genesis Record

The Book of Beginnings, Volume 1: Creation, Fall and the First Age

Articles at ICR.org

Evolution *Ex Nihilo*

Evolution, Thermodynamics, and Entropy

Can Order Come Out of Chaos?

Evolution Is Not Based on Natural Laws

The Ever-Changing Big Bang Story

"Smoking Gun" Evidence of Inflation?

Massive Black Hole Disrupts Galaxy Formation Theories

Study: Star Formation Is Virtually Finished

DVDs

Astronomy Reveals Creation

What You Aren't Being Told About Astronomy, Volumes 1–2

Created Cosmos

Episode 11

Books

The Solar System: God's Heavenly Handiwork

Guide to Creation Basics

Guide to Animals

The Young Earth

Exploring the Evidence for Creation

Creation Basics & Beyond

Articles at ICR.org

Earth: A Special Place

The Solar System: Earth and Moon

Scientist Suggests "We Are Actually All Martians"

Mars Even More Hostile to Life Than Previously Thought

Well-Engineered Ecosystems Bounce Back

Does Earth Balance Carbon Dioxide Levels Automatically?

Astronomers Speak: Our Solar System Is "Special"

DVD

What You Aren't Being Told About Astronomy, Volume 1

Episode 12

Books

Guide to Animals

Creation Basics & Beyond

Discerning Truth

The Ultimate Proof of Creation

Biblical Creationism

The Genesis Record

5 Reasons to Believe in Recent Creation

Biology and the Bible

Six Days of Creation

Exploring the Evidence for Creation

Guide to Creation Basics

The Book of Beginnings, Volumes 1–3

Articles at ICR.org

The Scientific Case Against Evolution

Things You May Not Know About Evolution

The Bible and/or Biology

The Vital Importance of Believing in Recent Creation

Why Should a Christian Believe in Creation?

Does the Phrase "Evening and Morning" Help Define "Day"?

Is the God of Theistic Evolution the Same as the God of the Bible?

Intelligent Design and/or Scientific Creationism

Episode 1 Answers

Brainy Buzzwords

Evidence You Can See

1. randomness, design
2. whale, bird, skeletons
3. categories, Carl Linnaeus, classification
4. mimicry, chameleon
5. theory of evolution, natural selection
6. common ancestor
7. Designer, complexity
8. beautiful, functional
9. adapt, cats, dogs, kind
10. DNA
11. selections
12. transitional, missing
13. evidence, species

Think Tank

1. (Answers may vary.) Hummingbirds have a unique design that allows them to hover, fly sideways, and fly backward. The mimic octopus can morph its body into 15 different creatures because of its design. Earth is perfectly suited for life—not too hot, not too cold. The bodies of animals are specially designed to suit their habitats. Birds have complex wings to help them fly. Elephants have trunks that can breathe, touch, and even grasp like a hand. My family members share similar traits and physical characteristics.

2. (Answers may vary.) God designed mimicry to allow creatures to blend in with their surroundings. The mimic octopus shows mimicry in the way that it can change its body to look like many different creatures. A chameleon can change its color to match its environment.

3. Beauty is there to showcase God's handiwork. He didn't have to make nature beautiful, but He did it for our enjoyment and His glory.

4. Evolutionists would say that life is the product of time, chance, and random changes.

5. Creation scientists would say that adaptation does happen but only within an animal's kind—like horses to zebras. Also, this adaptation doesn't come from an external source. It is built into the DNA of every living thing.

6. Evolutionists need evidence of transitional forms, but no undisputed evidence exists. Even secular scientists debate any fossil that is presented as a transitional form.

7. Answers will vary.

Back to the Bible

Respond

1. It took six days.

2. Day One: God created time (the beginning), space, (the heavens), matter (the earth), light energy (light), and the night-day cycle (Genesis 1:3-5). Day Two: He made the firmament (called heaven) and divided the waters (1:6-8). Day Three: He created dry land (Earth), the seas, and plants (1:9-13). Day Four: He made the sun, moon, and stars (1:14-19). Day Five: He made sea creatures and winged creatures (1:20-23). Day Six: He made land creatures and man (1:24-27).

3. God thought His creation was "very good" (Genesis 1:31).

4. God told His creation to "be fruitful and multiply," and He told man to "fill the earth and subdue it" and to have dominion over all other creatures (Genesis 1:22, 28).

5. God made man in His own image (Genesis 1:27).

6. (Answers may vary.) These verses tell us that God's purposes will stand. He's in control. He created with wisdom and understanding, is powerful, and has prepared us for good works. The God of the Bible is the only God—there are no others. God alone is all-powerful and responsible for creating everything we see, including distant galaxies and stars.

7. I can recognize His "invisible attributes…even His eternal power and Godhead" (Romans 1:20) in all of creation, for His design is apparent in everything He makes. And I can choose to obey Him and let His Word guide my daily life.

Episode 2 Answers

Brainy Buzzwords

Know Your Terms!
1. d.
2. e.
3. a.
4. f.
5. c.
6. b.

Alive or Not?
These are the items that should be circled: horse, rabbit, girl, bee, cow, lion, shark, roly-poly, butterfly

Think Tank

1. Scientists generally say that something is biologically alive if it has the ability (1) to move independently, (2) to metabolize, (3) to grow, (4) to adapt, and (5) to reproduce.

2. The Bible says that God created life and that man has a responsibility to rule over and care for Earth and its creatures.

3. The three mechanisms are adaptation, mutation, and natural selection.

4. (Answers may vary.) (1) Scientific experiments have never created life, but most evolutionary models require that spontaneous generation of life happened at least once in the beginning. (2) Vertical evolution relies on the pattern that simple life forms became complex, but there is no good explanation for that theory since mutations usually aren't beneficial. (3) Vertical evolution contradicts the Second Law of Thermodynamics. (4) The chicken-and-egg problem means that parts needed for life all depend on each other, so evolution can't explain how life started.

5. They demonstrated that life only comes from life.

6. Organisms bear "fruit according to [their] kind," with their seed in themselves. This indicates that God created organisms with the DNA to reproduce according to their own kind and not any other.

7. (Answers may vary.) If we are just the product of random chance, then God may not exist, life has no meaning, and standards of right and wrong have no basis.

8. Louis Pasteur performed experiments that showed that life only comes from life. Fred Hoyle said that if life were to come from non-life, it would be like a tornado sweeping through a junkyard and assembling a Boeing 747.

Back to the Bible

Respond

1. If you have blood, then you have life. It is a different definition from the ones many scientists use. Plants can metabolize and reproduce, but according to the Bible, they aren't alive in the same way that animals and people are alive because they don't have blood.

2. All of life came from God's creation of the world in Genesis 1.

3. (Answers may vary.) Humans were made in the image of God. Humans can make things out of their imaginations. Humans produce things purely for intellectual and aesthetic purposes. Humans are the only creatures that worship something.

4. God gave humans the responsibility of ruling over the world and caring for it.

5. (Answers may vary.) We can recognize that we are all made in the image of God, so we are all unique and special. We should treat each other with the high value God has given us.

6. Christians have hope in an eternal life spent with God through salvation in Jesus Christ.

Awesome Activities for All Ages

a. (1) Detect the sugar; (2) physically grasp sugar molecule; (3) transport molecule into cell without also transporting unwanted material; (4) "burn" the sugar to release its chemical energy; (5) capture that released energy; (6) store and/or deploy that captured energy

b. (Answers may vary.) Very tiny machinery; very precise machinery

c. Tiny but precise

d. (Answers may vary.) Ingenious, complicated, miniature

e. Chances are zero since yeast have no brains to design chemistry labs or any machines

Episode 3 Answers

Brainy Buzzwords

What's the Same and What's Different?
Students should circle any or all of these similarities:
  Ears, eyes, hooves, color of tail, color of body
Students should draw a square around any or all of these differences:
  Face markings, head shape/size, muzzle markings, leg markings, tail length, mane color, halter on mare

Cracking the Genetic Code

1. DNA, blueprint

2. macromolecule, nucleus, function

3. gene, gene

4. chromosome, generation

5. physical, hair, tall, characteristics, hair

6. organism, parent, one-cell

7. 23, mother, X, Y, gender, genetic, diseases

8. parent, grandparents, grandparents

9. molecule; ladder; [order may vary:] G, A, T, C; pair

10. genetic, sentences, paragraphs, chromosome

11. organism, human, zebra

Think Tank

1. Charles Darwin and Thomas Huxley helped form the idea of evolution. Their books divided science and theology (which actually agree) by suggesting that life had a natural cause not a divine cause.

2. Evolution's basic assumptions are (1) that all of life evolved over long spans of time, (2) that any differences among life forms are the result of natural selection and some adaptations and mutations along the way,

and (3) that similar design means that we must have a common ancestor.

3. It is commonly taught that the chimp and human genomes are 98-99 percent similar, but they are really only about 70 percent similar. Things like physical differences, dexterity, morality, and intellect also separate humans from chimps.

4. (1) None of the major steps of evolution have ever been repeated in a lab. (2) Evolution would happen too slowly for us to observe, and changes on the scale Darwin was suggesting have not been observed. (3) Evolution fails the test Darwin gave. It can be shown that many living organisms cannot be built by "numerous, successive, slight modifications" and so could not have evolved.

5. Calling a life system "irreducibly complex" means that to remove one part would destroy the function of the entire system. Irreducibly complex systems could not have been built by numerous, successive, slight modifications—or, in other words, evolution.

6. (Answers may vary.) Humans have many physical differences from chimps, such as the lack of overall body hair and a unique muscle in our forearm that allows us to be more creative with our hands. We also have emotional and intellectual differences from animals. Humans use complex language to communicate with each other and do many creative things. The biggest thing that sets humans apart is that we're created in God's image and with the ability to have fellowship with Him.

7. (Answers may vary.) Our view on origins matters because it affects what we believe about our meaning and purpose, our relationship with God, and our life after death.

8. (Answers may vary.) The Bible says that we are created in God's own image. This gives us value and meaning apart from animals.

Back to the Bible

Respond

1. God created man in His image. God works in us to make us more like Him and even died so that we could be forgiven and go to heaven. Animals do not receive this kind of attention from God or have fellowship with God.

2. God showed His love for us by sending His Son to die for our sins.

3. God has a special relationship with us by providing forgiveness and salvation and desiring companionship with us. Animals do not receive the benefits of this relationship.

4. (Answers may vary.) It means that God is helping us to become more like Him in the way we act and think. It means that as we grow closer to Him we should be more forgiving of others and more selfless in our motives and thoughts.

5. We were specially created by God in His image, and He sent Jesus to die to restore that relationship.

6. (Answers may vary.) People reject God and His commands and try to lead lives without meaning or purpose.

Episode 4 Answers

Brainy Buzzwords

Finding the Missing Links

```
I G L M E S S E V I D E N C E
O R G A N I S M O D T M E U S
L A N O I T I S N A R T S O T
S N A P S H O T R L N S I E R
W D N V A R S B N A I C B N A
M C E O I S E N C T H A H I T
E A O E I T D O T I O M R B A
L N C R R S M F G E A B U S O
X Y R E T P O E A H C R A M A
A O V A L S O L D S I I S U T
R N S E S L P A P A L A O D R
I I X I O F R R L X R N N F O
S H L G C W M R O F E F I L D
C S Y S I M P L E P O V D O N
D S K N I L G N I S S I M W O
```

Buried Evidence

1. fossils, layers, earth, deeper
2. fossils, evolved, buried, complex, upper, simple, slow
3. record, shift, organism
4. transitional, evidence
5. diversity, thousands, fossils, rapid, burial, decay
6. complexity, change, transitional, transitional, another
7. important

Think Tank

1. One of the main tools they use is the fossil record. Supposedly, it shows the gradual progression from simple to complex life forms and that, as you go deeper into Earth, you go deeper in time.

2. They say that creatures supposedly changed over long periods of time and so the fossil record should show evidences of those changes.

3. (Answers may vary.) Some scientists admit that evolution is an alternative to Christianity. Many see it as a belief system more than just a theory about origins—maybe because it requires faith.

4. The diversity of fossils is significant because it shows that many creatures were rapidly buried, likely by water. The stasis of fossils shows that life appeared fully formed and amazingly complex without any transitional forms.

5. The Cambrian layers are known for containing much more complex life than the Precambrian layers under it. This jump from hardly any fossils to many complex fossils is referred to as the Cambrian Explosion. This is an "unconformity" in the evolutionary model, and it contradicts the idea that the layers took millions of years to form.

6. Of the fossils we have, most are marine invertebrates. Less than one percent of the remaining five percent are vertebrates.

7. The fact that most fossils are the result of massive mudflows and rapid burial points to the Genesis Flood.

8. Soft tissue fossils cannot last for millions of years. The fact that soft tissue has been found in dinosaur bones that are supposedly 68 million years old indicates that dinosaurs may have lived just thousands of years ago.

9. (Answers may vary.) Galileo's claim was that the sun is at the center of our solar system, and Dr. Ignaz Philipp Semmelweis stressed the importance of hygiene in hospitals. Both were ridiculed by mainstream science, yet both turned out to be right. Just because people laugh at your beliefs doesn't mean you're wrong.

Back to the Bible

Respond

1. (Answers may vary.) Said, come, have seen, shall take, will cause, will destroy, have made, did, commanded, went, came, were broken up, were opened, entered, shut, increased, lifted, rose, prevailed, moved, were covered, died, destroyed, were destroyed, remained.

2. The ones that died were the "birds and cattle and beasts and every creeping thing that creeps on the earth, and every man" (Genesis 7:21). The ones that might have survived were the beasts of the seas, those that did not creep on the earth.

3. The fossil record shows diversity in its layers, indicating that many kinds of animals died at the same time by a great catastrophe. Also, all animals appear fully formed. This fits the Flood account.

4. It tells us that humans are not their own masters—God rules over us. Genesis is not a neutral book. We either choose to let the Word of God speak for itself, or we submit it to our own authority.

Episode 5 Answers

Brainy Buzzwords
Noah's Flood: A Truly Perfect Storm

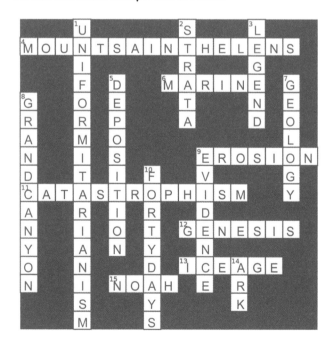

Did That Ark Float?

1. secularists, creationists, agreement
2. Flood, key
3. beliefs, evidence
4. uniformitarianism, processes, past
5. billions, time, changes, gradual, life, evolutionary
6. opposite, erosion, deposition, catastrophe, geological
7. catastrophism, Canyon, destructive, geologists, climate, short, Flood

Think Tank

1. *Catastrophism* is the view that the biblical account of the global Flood is accurate. The Flood caused most of the strata and fossils we see today in a very short time. Another view disregards the biblical account and believes changes to Earth's geology have been slow and gradual. This view is called *uniformitarianism*, and it holds that the processes we see today, like erosion and deposition, operated in the same way in the remote geological past—that there was no global catastrophe.

2. You get the idea of evolution. If rock strata took millions of years to form, then so did creatures.

3. They assume that "the present is the key to the past" and that today's geological processes are fully responsible for forming the geological layers, fossils, and rocks. According to this theory, the global Flood did not happen because Earth's materials and landforms that we see today are the result of slow and gradual processes.

4. The Flood took place about 4,500 years ago.

5. (Answers may vary.) The Flood was more than just a lot of heavy rain because it did a lot of geologic work in a very short amount of time. The Bible even says the fountains of the great deep were broken up at the beginning of the Flood. For a modern-day example of this kind of catastrophe, we can look at Mount St. Helens. Like the Flood, it did a lot of geologic work in a very short time, including carving a canyon and depositing rock layers.

6. The mountains were much smaller back then and were later uplifted by the collision of continental plates during the Flood to the heights they are now.

7. Much, if not most, of the Flood's water came from deep reservoirs the Bible calls the "fountains of the great deep" (Genesis 7:11). The ocean floors became hot, occupied more volume, and forced the world's sea level to rise.

8. All of the continents were once combined into a large supercontinent. At some point this continent broke apart into the continents we see today.

9. It shows that a catastrophe like the Flood could, in fact, do "millions of years" worth of geologic work in a short time.

Back to the Bible

Respond

1. These verses remind us of the doctrine of *uniformitarianism*.

2. He says that they are following their own sinful desires, questioning the promise of Jesus' coming, and choosing to forget God's creation and the Flood.

3. They willfully forget the Flood and creation by God's powerful and spoken word.

4. (Answers may vary.) Peter mentions the Flood because, if God judged the world once by water, then He can do it again by fire, as He promises. Peter is warning us that "in the last days" people will begin to deny that God is the Creator and will choose to forget key events like the Flood so they can pretend that their evil deeds won't be judged by a holy God.

5. (Answers may vary.) A good start is to ask them questions about what they believe about origins and why.

6. Just like He did for Noah, God provides a way of escape and rescue from destruction for us. The danger facing Noah was a worldwide Flood. For us, it's separation from God in hell. Jesus is the way of escape.

7. God's covenant with Noah was that He would never again destroy "every living creature" as He had done and that He would never again destroy the earth with a flood (Genesis 8:21; 9:11). This doesn't mean there will never again be a catastrophe.

Episode 6 Answers

Brainy Buzzwords

Earth: Young or Old?
1. VOLCANO
2. THOUSANDS
3. STRATA
4. ASSUMPTION
5. CARBON
6. CLOCK
7. RADIOACTIVE
8. PLANET
9. LIGHT
10. CONSTANT
11. DECAY
12. FAITH
13. FLOOD
14. LAYERS
15. MILLIONS
16. EVIDENCE
17. DARKNESS
18. CIVILIZATION
19. BIBLE
20. HISTORY
21. PROCESS
22. URANIUM
23. GEOCHRONOLOGY
24. TAPEATS
25. SCIENTIFIC

Age of Mystery?
1. history, human, see, conclusions
2. age, clues, faith
3. scientists, rocks
4. sand, constant
5. hourglass, time
6. Grand, uniform, fast
7. fast, carbon, fossils, thousands, rate
8. earth, millions, estimate, younger

Think Tank

1. All scientists look at chemical, biological, and physical clues.

2. The three assumptions are (1) a constant process rate, (2) a closed process system, and (3) a known initial process component.

3. They assume that the decay rate of uranium has always been the same.

4. There should be no detectable carbon-14 in fossils that are older than 100,000 years. And there should not be soft tissue or DNA in fossils dated at millions of years, but we still find it. Soft tissue and DNA can't survive for long periods of time. This suggests that those fossils were formed only thousands of years ago, not millions. Finds like these indicate Earth's layers might have been laid down quickly and recently by Noah's Flood.

5. The two main views are catastrophism, which says that it was formed fast by the watery catastrophe of Noah's Flood, and uniformitarianism, which says that it was carved gradually by the Colorado River over millions of years.

6. The Tapeats Sandstone occurs across North America and contains huge boulders that could only have been moved and deposited by a force like the Global Flood.

7. (Answers may vary.) Carbon-14 is routinely found in fossils that are in "multi-million-year-old" rock layers. However, carbon-14 cannot last longer than 100,000 years.

8. It matters because if the Bible is wrong or misleading in its opening chapters, then where else is it wrong?

Back to the Bible

Respond

1. (Answers may vary.) Day is connected to light. The evening and the morning make one day. God created in six days and rested on the seventh.

2. The Bible tells us that there was an "evening" and "morning" that made up each of the days. Exodus 20:11 and Exodus 31:17 also say that the creation work took six days.

3. If we cannot trust God's definition of a day in the opening chapter of His Word, then how can we trust anything else the Bible says?

4. The Hebrew word *yom* is translated as "day" in the Bible 1,167 times (the plural form is spelled *yamîm*). It is translated as "day" in the book of Genesis 127 times. Of those 127 uses in Genesis, *yom* is used 16 times in reference to creation. You should not find any instances in Genesis where it does not make sense for the word "day" (translated from *yom*) to be interpreted as a 24-hour day. (Note: This answer is based on *Young's Analytical Concordance to the Bible*.)

5. It tells us that God is logical and orderly and does not work in a way that would cause us to be uncertain or confused. Because of this, we can trust that the Genesis account is accurate. God told us how He made the universe in plain words that are clear and understandable.

Episode 7 Answers

Brainy Buzzwords

Disappearing Dinos: A History Mystery

1. Age, Mesozoic, 225, 66
2. Genesis, creatures, six, dinosaurs, powerful
3. a. structure, design, evolution, creation
   b. catastrophic, layer, rocks, fossils, floods, million, worldwide
   c. carbon
   d. soft, rocks, Mary Schweitzer, thighbone, million
   e. humans, writing, legends, world, stories, similar

Dino Hunt

```
U C S U C U A L A R B D S T
A O O P S S A A U O U I R A
S D O U U U G S A R S P O O
U T R U O A U A O U S L A L
R U E Y S S U Y R U S O A U
U G R G O O A U R R U D U S
A P A T O S A U R U S O P S
S U R U A S A R A M A C C R
O B A R O S A U R U S U B S
T R U D O A L U R A A S C P
P U Y L S U M D R U R O A A
M B L R O C R B D U S O A R
A A R U S A S D R U S S A I
C O A S R A A U A A A O G S
```

Think Tank

1. Secular scientists believe that dinosaurs lived before man millions of years ago, but creation scientists believe they lived at the same time as man and went extinct only a few thousand years ago.

2. The most popular theory is that an asteroid hit Earth and changed the climate and food supply, leading to the extinction of the dinosaurs.

3. Minerals begin to seep into its bones, changing their chemical composition. Once a fossil is exposed on Earth's surface, it starts to weather and must be retrieved before it disappears.

4. Dinosaurs and modern reptiles have different leg placements. Modern reptiles have legs that extend out to the side, which causes them to crawl. Many dinosaurs were much heavier, so their legs went straight down underneath them to support their weight.

5. The Morrison Formation, where Dinosaur National Monument is located, shows evidence of a catastrophe. (1) It is extensive—more so than we would expect from slow, gradual processes. (2) The formation is full of volcanic debris. (3) The formation contains fossils of both land and sea creatures mixed together.

6. Evidence of soft tissue in dinosaur fossils has challenged the assumption that they are millions of years old.

7. (Answers may vary.) The Bible says that animals and people were created at the same time, so we shouldn't be surprised when we find evidence that supports this.

8. (Answers will vary.) The Bible tells us that God created all animals within the same week that He created humans, and the book of Job even seems to describe a dinosaur. Soft tissue fossils support the idea that dinosaurs lived at the same time as humans, and dragon legends across the world suggest that eyewitnesses actually saw dinosaurs.

Back to the Bible

Respond

1. It indicates that dinosaurs lived at the same time as humans.

2. The behemoth's strength is in his hips, his power is in his stomach muscles, he moves his tail like a cedar, and the sinews of his thighs are tightly knit. We know that dinosaurs had very strong legs to support the weight of their body directly above. Some had giant, long tails. Because the behemoth's tail is compared to

a tree, this description would fit one of the larger dinosaurs. (Students may, from their research, know that the descriptions in Job match the modern descriptions of a sauropod.)

3. This verse makes it clear that death was the result of Adam and Eve's sin, so it was not present in creation before man. Explanations that say dinosaurs went extinct millions of years ago when an asteroid hit Earth suggest that death existed before man and do not fit the biblical timeline.

4. Revelation 21:4 tells us that we can look forward to a place where death is no more. This world of decay is passing, but Christians have hope of a world without pain and sorrow in eternity.

5. It will be a place where "righteousness dwells" (2 Peter 3:13).

Episode 8 Answers

Brainy Buzzwords

Unpacking the Layers

1. h. Aerosols
2. f. Debris
3. e. Glacial moraine
4. b. Glacier
5. g. Ice Age
6. c. Ice cores
7. a. Ice crystal
8. j. Ice sheet
9. i. Iceberg
10. d. Mt. Pinatubo

The Ice Age: Mystery, Madness, or Matter of Fact?

Think Tank

1. The biggest evidence we have for at least one ice age is the presence of *glacial moraines*, the debris fields of boulders, rocks, and dirt that indicate the paths of glaciers.

2. a. Uniformitarians say there were at least five major ice ages and as many as 50 smaller ones. Creationists say there was only one.
   b. Uniformitarians say that each ice age may have lasted tens of millions of years. Creationists say the Ice Age lasted only hundreds of years.
   c. Uniformitarians say that the last ice age began about 2.6 million years ago. Creationists say the one and only Ice Age began about 4,300 years ago.

3. Glaciers, ice cores, glacial moraines, and fossils, among other things.

4. Uniformitarians measure the ice cores based on the assumption that each layer of ice represents one year. However, the layers become more indistinct farther down. The flow models that are supposed to account for this are created with the assumption that the ice cores are millions of years old, so their results are not reliable.

5. No, because cold temperatures generally result in less, not more, snowfall.

6. The first thing needed is (1) **H**ot oceans which cause (2) **E**vaporation. More moisture in the air means more precipitation, including more snowfall at mid and high latitudes. (3) **A**erosols are also needed, which are released into the air by volcanic activity. The aerosols block the sun, and the result is cooler summers when the winter snow doesn't melt followed by winters when more snow falls. (4) **T**ime. Lastly, an ice age needs a short time to concentrate heat and aerosols.

7. The Flood would have caused massive storms, volcanism, earthquakes, and tectonic activity, heating up the oceans and causing the HEAT model to take effect. Modern-day examples are the eruption of Mt. Pinatubo on Luzon island in 1991 and the creation of Crater Glacier on Mount St. Helens just since 1980!

8. The Ice Age would not have been equally severe everywhere. In fact, there were probably many temperate areas in which humans could have lived.

Back to the Bible

Respond

1. He promised that He would never again "curse the ground for man's sake" or destroy every living thing as He had done (Genesis 8:21) and that He would never again destroy the earth with a flood (Genesis 9:11).

2. He gave the sign of a rainbow, and it represents His covenant that He would never send a flood again to destroy all flesh.

3. Land bridges would have aided humans in fulfilling God's command to "fill the earth" (Genesis 9:1).

4. (Answers may vary.) We can know that God keeps His promises, and this should increase our faith in His Word and covenants. He makes provisions for man to fulfill His commands and is trustworthy and good.

Extraordinary Evidence

Endnotes

1. Lutgens, F. K. and E. J. Tarbuck. 2010. *The Atmosphere: An Introduction to Meteorology,* 11th ed. New York: Prentice Hall, 145-146.

2. Warm summers in Siberia prevent glaciation despite very cold winter temperatures.

3. Genesis 7:11.

4. Woodmorappe, J. and M. Oard. 2002. Field studies in the Columbia River basalt, Northwest USA. *Journal of Creation*. 16 (1): 103-110.

5. Silvestru, E. 2001. The Permian extinction: *National Geographic* comes close to the truth. *Journal of Creation.* 15 (1): 6-8.

6. Vardiman, L. 2001. *Climates Before and After the Genesis Flood.* San Diego, CA: Institute for Creation Research, 60.

7. Vardiman, L. 1998. Numerical Simulation of Precipitation Induced by Hot Mid-Ocean Ridges. In *Proceedings of the Fourth International Conference on Creationism.* Pittsburgh, PA: Creation Science Fellowship, 595-605.

8. de Castella, T. 2010. The eruption that changed Iceland forever. *BBC News Magazine.* Posted on news.bbc.co.uk April 16, 2010.

9. Oard, M. 1990. *An Ice Age Caused by the Genesis Flood.* San Diego, CA: Institute for Creation Research, 93-117.

10. Osgood, J. 1981. The Date of Noah's Flood. *Journal of Creation.* 4 (1): 10-13.16. Oard, M. 2000. The extinction of the woolly mammoth: was it a quick freeze? Journal of Creation. 14 (3): 24-34.

11. Oard, M. 2000. The extinction of the woolly mammoth: was it a quick freeze? *Journal of Creation.* 14 (3): 24-34.

12. Oard, M. 2004. *Frozen in Time.* Green Forest, AR: Master Books.

Episode 9 Answers

Brainy Buzzwords

The Human Family Tree

Answers from Archaeology

1. 1800, Baghdad, ruins, cuneiform, Chaldeans, Abraham, mythical, evidence, Bible
2. Tablets, Ebla, fragments, Bible, Gomorrah
3. cultures, archaeologists, 150, Babylon, thrived, 4,000

Think Tank

1. After Darwin presented his evolutionary theory, Thomas Huxley applied it to people by writing a book that showed what he thought were the similarities between humans and apes.

2. Secular scientists believe that humans and chimps share a common ancestor. In this scenario, roughly eight million years ago in Africa, humans began to evolve and diverge from their apelike ancestors. Over six million years ago, humans began to walk upright, use tools, migrate out of Africa, and develop language. Within the past 100,000 years or so, those advanced apes became modern humans.

3. The secular scientists call them *mitochondrial Eve* and *Y-chromosome Adam*. These supposed progenitors of the human race were part of a larger population rather than two specific individuals. This is different from the Bible's account that says the progenitors of the human race (the *real* Adam and Eve) were the only ones of their kind.

4. They say that ancient humans migrated around the globe, in part due to changes in climate and food supply. As humans dispersed, different races began to appear as we became more genetically diverse—for example, darker coloration in warmer climates and lighter coloration in the north.

5. The secular "Great Leap Forward" was the supposed development of symbolic and written language some 40,000 to 50,000 years ago.

6. Many evidences of places mentioned in the Bible have been found and excavated, such as the famous Ziggurat of Ur, the Tablets of Ebla (which mention Sodom and Gomorrah), Nineveh, and Babylon. These discoveries support the Bible's history as an accurate record.

7. God's confusion of speech at the Tower of Babel led to the different languages. God then scattered humanity abroad over the earth.

8. Variation was created in humans from the beginning. The *founder principle* in genetics suggests that the segregation of mankind into small, inbreeding family units would have rapidly generated distinctive physical characteristics associated with each tribe. The genetic and geographic isolation would also lead to each tribe developing its own culture, tools, and way of life.

9. The emphasis on differences comes from man, not the Bible. The theory of evolution leads dangerously to the idea that some races are more advanced than others.

Back to the Bible

Respond

1. Acts 17:26 says God made us all from one blood and determined our times and geographic locations. He is involved and has a plan.

2. The ultimate cause was man's arrogance.

3. The Bible says that we are all descended from Noah's sons Shem, Ham, and Japheth. In many people groups, we find oral traditions and written memories of pre-Babel events—evidence that all of humanity shared those experiences and were subsequently scattered. Beginning with Noah's sons, if you use a modest growth rate, then you can arrive at a number that is even greater than today's population. It's realistic that all humanity came from Noah's family.

4. We should view that kind of prejudice as sinful because God has made everyone in His image with great worth and value (Psalm 139:14).

Awesome Activities 5

Modern Place Name	Alternative / Ancient Place Name	Extinct Culture?	Genesis 10 Verse	Genesis 10 Leader Name
Egypt	Mizr	N	6	Mizraim
Assyria	Asshur	Y	22	Asshur
Hebrew (Israel)	Eber	N	21	Eber
Ethiopia (approx.)	Cush	N	6	Cush
Birs Nimrud	Tower of Babel	Y	8	Nimrod
Palestine	Philistia	N	14	Pathrusim
Wales	Cambria (Cymru)	N	2	Gomer
Greece	Ionia	N	2	Javan
Dardanelles	Dardania	N	4	Dodanim
Tblisi, Georgia	Tiflis	N	2	Tubal
Tobolsk, Russia	N/A	N	2	Tubal

Extraordinary Evidence

Endnotes

1. Ayala, F. 1978. The Mechanisms of Evolution. *Scientific American*. 239 (3): 56-69.

Episode 10 Answers

Brainy Buzzwords

Lots of Laws

1. b. The Law of Increasing Entropy
2. e. The Law of Cause and Effect
3. a. Sir Isaac Newton
4. f. Potential energy
5. c. Kinetic energy
6. m. First Law of Thermodynamics
7. k. George LeMaitre
8. h. Edwin Hubble
9. d. Cosmic Microwave Background Radiation (CMB)
10. l. The Big Bang
11. n. Planck satellite
12. i. Blue stars
13. g. Spiral galaxies
14. j. Cosmic inflation

Space Scramble

1. ASTEROID
2. WHITE DWARF
3. SOLAR ECLIPSE
4. NOVA
5. MILKY WAY
6. METEOR

7. CONSTELLATION
8. SPIRAL GALAXY
9. RED DWARF
10. FIREBALL
11. COMET
12. GALACTIC DISK
13. PLANET
14. NEBULA
15. BLACK HOLE
16. DWARF GALAXY
17. MOON
18. STAR
19. SUPERNOVA
20. MICROWAVES
21. ELLIPTICAL GALAXY

Think Tank

1. Empirical science has to do only with the observable present. What happened in the past is not something we can test directly. This means that we have to take what we know in the present and work backward to understand our origins. At some level, faith is required, and all we can do is take the evidence we have and try to come to the best conclusion.

2. (Answers may vary.) The laws of physics demonstrate the order and precision of creation, and God gave them to us so we could understand our world and His nature. Science would be disorderly and illogical without them.

3. The Big Bang theory says that the entire universe began as a point, a singularity, which rapidly expanded and caused everything we see today.

4. Secular scientists thought the microwave radiation was leftover from the Big Bang. The Big Bang theory predicts that there would be hot and cold spots in the universe, showing variations in the CMB temperature. However, new research has shown that the CMB temperature is much more uniform than scientists predicted. These variations also contradict Big Bang predictions by suggesting a special direction in space.

5. (Answers may vary.) The laws of physics show that order does not come from chaos. Gravity holds the sun's hydrogen together. A block of wood falling on a table transitions from potential to kinetic energy and shows the First Law of Thermodynamics: Energy cannot be created or destroyed, only converted. These laws are consistent and predictable.

6. (Answers may vary.) The Second Law of Thermodynamics shows a universal tendency for things to go toward a state of equilibrium (same temperature everywhere) in which no energy is available to do work. But the Big Bang is supposed to have started in such a state. How then could we possibly have non-equilibrium conditions today? How do we have usable energy today if the universe started in such a state?

Back to the Bible

Respond

1. (Answers may vary.) Genesis 1 tells us that the universe was created by the spoken words of God. Genesis 8:22 shows us that God intended creation to be orderly and regular, not chaotic. Psalm 74:16 shows us that God not only created the universe but that He also holds authority over it. Isaiah 40:26 tells us God commands and preserves the heavenly hosts.

2. God created space, time, matter, and energy on the first day of creation.

3. The First Law of Thermodynamics states that energy cannot be created or destroyed, simply converted.

The amount of original energy created by God is the same today as in the beginning and had to be instilled in the universe by an outside force.

4. The Law of Conservation of Mass and Energy (the First Law of Thermodynamics) states that energy can be transferred from one form to another, but not created or destroyed. These verses support this by saying that God's creation will endure because He is upholding it by His power.

5. The universe can't be eternally old because all the energy in it would have been degraded into a totally useless form by now.

6. We know from simple logic that every beginning requires a cause. The law that applies to this is called The Law of Cause and Effect.

7. God is not changeful or unstable. We can know that the universe and laws of physics are under His control. We can trust God to be constant and trustworthy, and this applies to the promises He has made regarding our lives and salvation.

Episode 11 Answers

Brainy Buzzwords

Life on Other Planets?
1. seven, sun, solar, spiral, Milky, 400, light, galaxy
2. terrestrial, rock, Venus, Mars
3. giants, Saturn, Neptune, Pluto, dwarf
4. Earth, life
5. Mercury, sun, life
6. size, carbon, life
7. long, smaller, thin, water
8. gas, evidence
9. cold, lifeless
10. giants, Pluto, life

Earth: No Place Like Home

1. JUPITER
2. PLUTO
3. SATURN
4. GAS GIANT
5. SPHERICAL
6. FLARE
7. EARTH
8. ORBIT
9. SPACECRAFT
10. MARS
11. TELESCOPE
12. VENUS
13. DWARF PLANET
14. ASTRONOMY
15. TILT
16. GALAXY
17. URANUS
18. EXPLOSION
19. NEPTUNE
20. MILKY WAY
21. PLANET
22. MOON
23. SOLAR SYSTEM
24. MERCURY
25. GOLDILOCKS ZONE

Think Tank

1. The planets closest to the sun are called terrestrial planets because they're composed mostly of rock and metals: Mercury, Venus, Earth, and Mars. The four outer planets are called gas giants because they're made primarily of gas and frozen vapor: Jupiter, Saturn, Uranus, and Neptune.

2. This is the area not so close to the sun that the oceans on a planet boil away and not so far from the sun that the oceans freeze—where secular scientists think there may be planets (besides Earth) with conditions necessary for life.

3. Water. Liquid water on its own is not enough to build life, even though life requires liquid water.

4. Scientists believe it is a planet in the Goldilocks zone that they think may have the right conditions for sustaining life.

5. (Answers may vary.) Mercury has no atmosphere and is too hot because it is so close to the sun. Venus has a dense, hot atmosphere that's mostly carbon dioxide. Mars' atmosphere is too thin to sustain life. Jupiter is just a big ball of gas, and we've found no evidence of life on any of its moons. Saturn is a cold sphere of gas, and its moons appear to be barren, lifeless places. Uranus and Neptune are poisonous gas giants, too.

6. (Answers may vary.) (1) Water: We're at the right spot for water to exist in the liquid state. If Earth's orbit were as extreme as many of the planets outside our solar system, then oceans would boil at the closest point and freeze at the farthest. (2) Atmosphere: With the perfect thickness to allow life, Earth's atmosphere protects the earth from some cosmic radiation. This includes some ultraviolet radiation that is blocked by a layer of ozone and oxygen that keeps UV light from damaging living cells. (3) Magnetic field: Earth's protective magnetic field deflects charged cosmic radiation, but this field is not so strong that it would radiate and kill living organisms. (4) Tilt: Earth's tilt, at 23.4 degrees on its axis, is also well suited for life. If our planet were tilted less, we wouldn't have as many livable regions. And if the tilt were greater, seasons would become too extreme.

7. There's just no hard evidence that any of the other planets are capable of sustaining life.

8. (Answers may vary.) If you don't believe in special creation, then that can also mean that humans are not special. There is no unique value and worth to our planet and the life on it if we believe Earth is just one of many things in the universe that "just happened." If people don't have worth, then there is no reason to protect life or live a purposed life, and there is no hope in God or salvation in Jesus, His Son.

9. Answers should involve some of the observations from the answers to question 6, with perhaps some physical observations students may make about the world around them.

Back to the Bible

Respond

1. To be inhabited. He created it for people!

2. The earth is round and "hangs on nothing." When the Bible tells us that the earth is round, that's exactly what we see. It is also suspended in space, just as God says when He describes the earth as hanging on nothing.

3. God tells us that the sun was created to rule the day and the moon was created to rule the night. And this is what we see happening in our solar system today.

4. Five days. Because He spent five days working on it and only one day for everything else, God emphasized Earth's uniqueness.

5. (Answers may vary.) God created everything—the heavens and the earth. He established it. He did not create in vain. He created with purpose—the sun and moon and stars were given special jobs. He intended the earth to be inhabited. He placed things exactly where He wanted them to be in space. He gave His creations special names. He created everything in a state that He considered good.

6. He saw that it was good.

7. God was intentional with His creation and satisfied with it. His attention to detail shows how much He cares about us. Because of the great care God showed when He created—and knowing in addition that we are created in His image—we should give our planet and our fellow man respect, value, and importance. We should view life as having great significance.

Extraordinary Evidence

Endnotes

1. Earth reaches perihelion (its closest point to the sun) around January 3, at which time our planet is 91.4 million miles away from the sun. In early July, Earth reaches aphelion (its farthest distance from the sun) at a distance of 94.5 million miles.

2. Baumgardner, J. R. 1994. Runaway Subduction as the Driving Mechanism for the Genesis Flood. In *Proceedings of the Third International Conference on Creationism*. R. E. Walsh, ed. Pittsburg, PA: Creation Science Fellowship, 63-86.

Episode 12 Answers

Brainy Buzzwords

Beginnings Matter

1. designed, accident, life, life, die, purpose

2. world, reason, meaning

3. creatures, design, Designer

4. Bible, life, beginning, earth, land, herbs, night, years, moon, winged, man, good

5. Genesis, system, big, chemical, soup

6. death, purpose, man, gift, eternal, Lord

The Big Picture

```
S C O F F E R S I S O T M R N V L
S A O V N R A L U C E S N I R I L
E L N V S W O R L D V I E W M S Y
S R A C E T M N I Y I T S A T N S
A U C O E N N E E G P N G I S E D
S Y P C F S A E A O B E L I E V E
V S V E U A T N T L C I M S O C E
L N S S R W U O T O A C S S T R E
D G I E C N R G R E P S E R H E T
T I N R N T A F I A U I A N E B S
N E V E I T L T B H E N N O O A E
S R I E E O I T U C M M D M L S O
M E S N R C S W T R E O T I O E B
O V I R L S T U E A A E D P G I I
G O B O A N I O S Y G L R N I E V
E S L O Y E C T O A E U N I A R G
T N E D I C C A Y D P E S I N R L
```

Think Tank

1. (Answers may vary.) Creation is supported by both scientific evidence and the Bible. Evolutionary theories contradict the Bible and are discredited by actual scientific evidence. The secular world sees evolution as "real" science, and it is taught more commonly than creation. People often believe what they hear the most. Many are not aware of the evidence that discredits evolutionary theory. It is also a spiritual battle—even when presented with truth, people don't want to believe it. The Bible describes how people will resist the idea of believing in God and His work (Romans 1:20; 2 Peter 3:5).

2. With evolution, instead of God you have natural forces being viewed as the cause of everything—these processes make mistakes and have to keep trying again until things turn out right. The evolutionary model relies on long ages of time and lots of death to explain origins. For creationists, God created life and He created man in His own image—no mistakes. Death originally started in the garden when Adam and Eve introduced sin into a perfect world. Everything "not good" about creation exists because after sin things could not be perfect anymore.

3. Humans were directly created "in the image of God," different from animals, and have a unique ability to have a personal relationship with the One who gave them His own "likeness." This image of God can be seen when humans work together to build, think, and create at a level chimpanzees never have and when we do great, complex things like send men to the moon. There are also significant physical differences between humans and chimps.

4. It contradicts the evolutionary belief that Earth is billions of years old and that life evolved over long ages. The evidence indicates that Noah's Flood could have produced the fossil record and laid down Earth's geological strata (layers) in a much shorter time than the millions of years that is taught. The Flood also marks the beginning of the Second Age of Earth's history that will end one day, as promised.

5. Because Adam sinned, death entered the world. Humans didn't begin hundreds of millions of years ago—everyone agrees on that. So if you believe that fossils are that old, then you believe that death came before man—it would already have been around when Adam sinned. So, why would Jesus have to die to save us if death was not really our penalty? What we believe about the timing of creation actually connects to our need for salvation through Jesus Christ and how we view the Bible's accuracy.

6. When God refers to creation in Genesis He uses the Hebrew word *yom*, which is translated as "day" in connection with creation and makes sense to be understood as a 24-hour day. He also says that the evening and the morning made up the first day, which perfectly matches the way our days work according to Earth's rotation.

7. If we cannot trust what God says about the timing of creation in the first book of the Bible, then we have to wonder what other parts of Scripture should not be trusted.

8. Answers may vary but could include: This view denies God's existence and authority and the laws of nature that He put into place. It says humans make the rules, and there is nothing higher than man. There are no objective standards that give life purpose, define what is right and wrong, give reasons to treat our Earth and fellow humans with respect, or demand accountability. The idea that "anything goes" leans toward chaos and not toward the order and design that God the Creator placed within His creation and His plan for eternity.

Back to the Bible

Respond

1. Evidence shows that at a modest growth rate the world population could get to today's size and genetic diversity in about 4,500 years, from just Noah and his three sons. Archaeological discoveries and historical writings verify many of the people and places in the Bible, like the Tower of Babel and its wicked leader Nimrod. There is strong evidence that the 70 original major language groups stem from when God confused language at the Tower of Babel.

2. God is the Creator! He made two great lights and the stars. The heavens declare His glory and the firmament shows His work. The sun, moon, and stars each have their own glory, and each star is unique, showing that God created with a careful plan.

3. Jesus was telling Nicodemus that if people wouldn't believe what He said about earthly things, then they wouldn't believe Him about heavenly things. This is why details about how long it took God to create the world matter! Evidence supporting that God created everything in six days matters because if that is not true, the heavenly things of the Bible—like salvation—can be questioned too.

4. A worldview is the belief system through which someone views everything about life. It is the framework for how they see the world and determines their actions, priorities, and expectations. (Answers may vary concerning personal worldview.)

5. The evidence for God as Creator is readily available, so people do not have an excuse for denying Him.

6. Peter said people "willfully forget" the evidence that is directly in front of them—that God created the heavens and the earth. When people say "all things continue as they were from the beginning of creation" this describes the uniformitarian or naturalistic worldview that claims that the geological processes we see today operated in the same way in the past.

7. (Answers may vary.) The naturalistic worldview exalts nature and man and attempts to explain the existence and nature of everything without God. The creationist worldview acknowledges God as Creator, King of everything, and the One who gives us salvation through Jesus Christ—we exist to glorify Him. By excluding God, the naturalistic worldview denies the essence of our purpose and identity as humans and devalues our world and our universe by attributing everything we see to just a cosmic accident.

8. God is above all, and everything we have is a gift from Him. We should respond by giving Him all glory, praise, and thanks and by taking good care of the earth He has given to us!

Bonus Episode Answers

Brainy Buzzwords

Now and Then
1. zero, earth
2. 1,056
3. 1,536, Ark
4. Flood, 371
5. Ice Age, 300
6. God, Tower of Babel, language
7. 2100, father, Ur
8. Egypt, pyramids
9. 4,000, Lord

* Dates are approximations. "There are considerable uncertainties in calculations." Some creation scientists estimate that the Ice Age "lasted for about 700 years." (See page 67.)

Index

Acknowledgments

SERIES HOST
Unlocking the Mysteries of Genesis *host Markus Lloyd is a professional actor. He received his B.F.A. in theater/television from Texas Christian University.*

SCIENCE EXPERTS

Mark Armitage, M.S., Ed.S.
Mr. Armitage received his M.S. in biology at the Institute for Creation Research Graduate School in San Diego, California, and his Ed.S. in science education from Liberty University.

John Baumgardner, Ph.D.
Dr. Baumgardner received his M.S. in electrical engineering from Princeton University and his M.S. and Ph.D. in geophysics and space physics from the University of California, Los Angeles.

Leslie P. Bruce, Ph.D.
Dr. Bruce received his M.A. in biblical education from Columbia Bible College and his Ph.D. in linguistics from Australian National University.

Vernon R. Cupps, Ph.D.
Dr. Cupps received his Ph.D. in nuclear physics from Indiana University Bloomington.

Randy Guliuzza, P.E., M.D.
Dr. Guliuzza received his B.S. in engineering from the South Dakota School of Mines and Technology, his M.D. from the University of Minnesota, and his M.P.H. from Harvard University.

Jake Hebert, Ph.D.
Dr. Hebert received his Ph.D. in physics from the University of Texas at Dallas.

Nathaniel T. Jeanson, Ph.D.
Dr. Jeanson received his Ph.D. in cell and developmental biology from Harvard University.

James J. S. Johnson, J.D., Th.D.
Dr. Johnson received his J.D. from the University of North Carolina and his Th.D. from Emmanuel College of Christian Studies.

Jason Lisle, Ph.D.
Dr. Lisle received his Ph.D. in astrophysics from the University of Colorado.

John D. Morris, Ph.D.
Dr. Morris received his Ph.D. in geological engineering from the University of Oklahoma.

Georgia Purdom, Ph.D.
Dr. Purdom received her Ph.D. in molecular genetics from Ohio State University.

Frank Sherwin, M.A.
Mr. Sherwin received his M.A. in zoology from the University of Northern Colorado.

Brian Thomas, M.S.
Mr. Thomas received his M.S. in biotechnology from Stephen F. Austin State University.

Jeffrey Tomkins, Ph.D.
Dr. Tomkins received his M.S. in plant science from the University of Idaho and his Ph.D. in genetics from Clemson University.

Larry Vardiman, Ph.D.
Dr. Vardiman received his Ph.D. in atmospheric science from Colorado State University.

John Whitmore, Ph.D.
Dr. Whitmore received his M.S. in geology from the Institute for Creation Research Graduate School and his Ph.D. in biology from Loma Linda University.

***Unlocking the Mysteries of Genesis** was filmed at the following locations:*
AMS Pictures, Dallas, Texas
Auto City Salvage, Dallas, Texas
Collin County Courthouse, McKinney, Texas
Dinosaur National Monument, Utah
Fort Worth Botanic Garden, Fort Worth, Texas
George Observatory, Needville, Texas
Grand Canyon, Arizona
Institute for Creation Research, Dallas, Texas
Lake Lewisville, Lewisville, Texas
Matanuska Glacier, Alaska
Texas Discovery Gardens, Dallas, Texas
Victory Bible Camp & Conference Center, Sutton, Alaska

***Unlocking the Mysteries of Genesis** was produced by the* **Institute for Creation Research in association with AMS Pictures.**

Executive Producer Tim Wylie
Senior Producer Charlotte Spivey
Director Steve Feldman
Content Director Laura Neitzel

Project supervision provided by the Institute for Creation Research.

Executive Team
Dr. Henry M. Morris III, Chief Executive Officer
Eileen Turner, Chief Financial Officer
Jayme Durant, Director of Communications

Development Team
Christian Staley, Student Guide Development Editor
Susan Windsor, Student Guide Designer
James Turner, Media Production Engineer

Special thanks to the entire staff of the Institute for Creation Research for backing this great adventure with sacrificial work and faithful prayers.

Dear Viewer,

Thank you for choosing the *Unlocking the Mysteries of Genesis Student Guide* as a teaching resource.

For over four decades, the Institute for Creation Research has been dedicated to scientific research for the purpose of equipping believers with evidence of the Bible's accuracy and authority. Through books, articles, films, DVDs, devotionals, speaking events, radio, and social media, we have been committed to sharing the science supporting the truth of God's creation.

Newer generations, disillusioned by unanswered questions, are leaving the faith in waves. We want to give them answers. The result? The development of *Unlocking the Mysteries of Genesis,* a powerful 12-DVD series designed to show how science and faith reveal the same truth.

And this is a truth we are passionate about for good reason. As a research organization, ICR conducts laboratory, field, theoretical, and library research on projects that seek to understand the science of origins and Earth history. Our scientists have conducted multi-year research projects at key locations like Grand Canyon, Mount St. Helens, Yosemite Valley, and Santa Cruz River Valley in Argentina, and on vital issues like Radioisotopes and the Age of the Earth (RATE), Flood-Activated Sedimentation and Tectonics (FAST), BioOrigins, soft-tissue fossils, and other topics related to biology, geology, genetics, astrophysics, geophysics, paleoclimatology, zoology, physics, and more. Everywhere we turn, the data show the undeniable purpose and plan of the Great Designer.

Additionally, through our School of Biblical Apologetics (SOBA), we offer multiple degree programs, training men and women in real-world apologetics, with a foundation of biblical authority and creation science.

We hope that your journey through *Unlocking the Mysteries of Genesis* has shown you clearly how scientific evidence confirms the biblical account of creation, affirmed your faith, and provided you with defensible answers to some of the most controversial issues of faith and science!

But don't let it stop there. Share it with the world, and join us in proclaiming the truth of God's creation.

For His glory,
Dr. Henry M. Morris III, CEO

P. O. Box 59029
Dallas, Texas 75229
www.ICR.org

800.337.0375 (main) | 800.628.7640 (customer service)

Get more facts with *Guide to Creation Basics* and *Guide to Animals*! Designed for all ages, these hardcover books are loaded with cutting-edge scientific information and hundreds of full-color illustrations.

To order, call **800.628.7640** or visit **www.icr.org/store**

Also available for Kindle, Nook, and through the iBookstore